uthors
In
Depth

. . . .

BRONZE LEVEL

PRENTICE HALL
Upper Saddle River, New Jersey
Glenview, Illinois
Needham, Massachusetts

ISBN 0-13-052384-4

6 7 8 9 10   04 03

PRENTICE HALL

Acknowledgments

Grateful acknowledgment is made to the following for copyrighted material:

Arte Publico Press
"A Voice," "Divisadero Street, San Francisco," and "Stubborn Woman" by Pat Mora from *COMMUNION*. Copyright © 1991 by Pat Mora. "Same Song" by Pat Mora from *BORDERS*. Copyright © 1986 Pat Mora.

Four Winds Press/Bradbury Press
"A Bad Road for Cats" and "Planting Things" by Cynthia Rylant from *EVERY LIVING THING*. Copyright © 1985 by Cynthia Rylant.

Harcourt Inc.
"Ode to Pomegranates" by Gary Soto from *LIVING UP THE STREET: NARRATIVE RECOLLECTIONS*. Text copyright © 1992 by Gary Soto. "The No-Guitar Blues" by Gary Soto from *BASEBALL IN APRIL AND OTHER STORIES*. Copyright © 1990 by Gary Soto. "Ballet folklorico" by Gary Soto from *CANTO FAMILIAR*. Copyright © 1995 by Gary Soto.

Barbara Hogenson Agency
"Canines in the Cellar" and "Memorial" by James Thurber from *THURBER'S DOGS: A COLLECTION OF THE MASTER'S DOGS, WRITTEN AND DRAWN, REAL AND IMAGINARY, LIVING AND LONG AGO*. All rights reserved including the right of reproduction in whole or in part in any form. Copyright © 1926, 1927, 1928, 1929, 1930, 1931, 1932, 1933, 1934, 1935, 1936, 1937, 1938, 1939, 1940, 1941, 1942, 1943, 1944, 1945, 1946, 1947, 1948, 1949, 1950, 1951, 1952, 1953, 1954, 1955, by James Thurber. Published by Simon and Schuster, Inc. From "The Pet Department" by James Thurber from *THE THURBER CARNIVAL*. Copyright © 1931, 1932, 1933, 1935, 1936, 1937, 1938, 1939, 1940, 1942, 1943, 1945, by James Thurber. All rights reserved.

Acknowledgments continue on page 182.

Contents

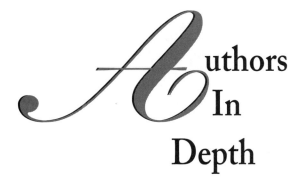

Authors In Depth

. . . .

BRONZE LEVEL

$\mathcal{G}$ary Soto In Depth

"For me, the joy of being a writer is to take things I see and hear and then rearrange them. I like to tamper with reality and create new possibilities"

—Gary Soto

GARY SOTO writes award-winning poems and stories that are both unique and universal. Their sharp observations reflect his insightful view of Mexican American culture. However, the natural emotions they evoke can be shared by readers of all backgrounds.

A California Childhood Soto grew up in Fresno, California, where his parents and grandparents worked in nearby packing houses, factories, and farms. When he was five, his family moved to a Mexican American neighborhood in outer Fresno. Soon after, Soto's father died in a factory accident. Soto and his siblings were raised by their mother and grandparents.

Although his neighborhood was poor, Soto loved it deeply. The settings and experiences of his youth would eventually inspire many of his poems and stories.

As a boy, Soto preferred baseball and basketball to reading and writing. There were few indications that Soto would grow up to be a well-known writer; in fact, he and his family read very little. "I don't think I had any literary aspirations when I was a kid," Soto remembers. "We didn't have books, and no one encouraged us to read."

Discovery in the Library Amazingly, Soto can remember the exact moment that his interest in reading and writing began. He was a geography major at Fresno City College, and he needed to research a report on continental drift. "I went to the library but dreaded the idea of looking up 'sources,'" he recalls, "so I just walked around doing nothing until I spotted a poetry anthology that looked interesting." That book, *The New American Poetry,* edited by Donald Allen, would change Soto's life forever.

Soto says that the poems seemed to leap off the page. One poem, called "Unwanted," by Edward Field, had a particularly strong effect. It is about alienation, or feeling like you don't belong. Soto recognized himself in Field's description, and reading the poem helped him to feel less alone.

Excited by his discovery, Soto spent the next few weeks reading poetry. Soon, he wanted to express his own ideas in writing.

A Poet Branches Out At first, Soto wrote only poetry. His first collection, *The Elements of San Joaquin,* was published in 1977, and the next year, he published *The Tale of Sunlight.* His poetry won many awards, and Soto became a professor of English and Ethnic Studies at the University of California.

In 1985, Soto decided to broaden his career as a writer. In *Living Up the Street,* he wrote short stories about growing up in Fresno. Even though the forms are very different, Soto saw a strong connection between his stories and his poems. "I made a conscious effort not to tell anything but just present the stories and let the reader come up with the assumptions about the book—just show not tell, which is what my poetry has been doing for years."

Writing for a New Audience After writing about his youth, Soto found that writing for young people was a natural step. In *Baseball in April and Other Stories* (1990), Soto depicts daily life in a Mexican American community. This highly successful collection was followed by two novels, *Taking Sides* (1991) and *Pacific Crossing* (1992), that tell the story of Lincoln Mendoza. These books trace the challenges Lincoln faces while learning to value, rather than hide, his Mexican American heritage. Soto returns to the theme of cultural pride in many of his stories.

Memory and Imagination Keeping the past alive is an important part of Soto's writing. He was deeply saddened when many of the buildings in his childhood neighborhood were torn down in the 1960's. He says that much of his writing is a reaction to the loss of this happy childhood place.

Although he is inspired by events and people from his past, many of Soto's details come from his imagination. He knows that readers often think his work is autobiographical because he writes a lot about growing up as a Mexican American. However, he explains that "as a writer, I like to make things up, as long as the actions of the characters are believable." Soto often combines real and imagined details to create "a story that becomes alive and meaningful in the reader's mind."

Encouraging New Readers and Writers In addition to writing, Soto loves to meet his readers. He enjoys playing baseball and basketball with the young people he meets at schools, and he hopes that his visits will excite students about reading and writing. "I figure if they meet me, they will be curious to read what I write," he says. "If that inspires them to read what other people write, all the better!"

◆ The Barrio

Gary Soto grew up in the *barrio,* which is a Spanish word that means "neighborhood." Often, a barrio is a Spanish-speaking area. Soto's barrio was on the outskirts of Fresno; there are other barrios in Los Angeles, San Diego and many cities in the United States.

Not all people who speak Spanish share the same ethnic or cultural background. For example, people from Spain, Mexico, and Nicaragua have very different customs and world views. Barrios often include people from a single cultural background, such as Soto's Mexican American barrio in Fresno.

Soto acknowledges these differences when he advises authors against writing about "the whole Latino experience." He suggests that, instead, writers should try to capture their own local experience. "I happen to be Mexican American, and I can only write about that one segment of Latino people," he says. "I can't write about Cuban Americans, Puerto Ricans, and so forth."

◆ Literary Works

Poetry
- *A Fire in My Hands: A Book of Poems* (1991)
- *Neighborhood Odes* (1992)
- *Canto Familiar/Familiar Song* (1995)

Short Stories
- *Baseball in April and Other Stories* (1990)
- *Local News* (1993)

Novels
- *Taking Sides* (1991)
- *Pacific Crossing* (1992)
- *Jesse* (1994)
- *Buried Onions* (1997)
- *Nickel and Dime* (2000)

Non-Fiction
- *Living Up the Street* (1985)
- *Small Faces* (1986)
- *A Summer Life* (1990)

The No-Guitar Blues

The moment Fausto saw the group Los Lobos on "American Bandstand," he knew exactly what he wanted to do with his life—play guitar. His eyes grew large with excitement as Los Lobos ground out a song while teenagers bounced off each other on the crowded dance floor.

He had watched "American Bandstand" for years and had heard Ray Camacho and the Teardrops at Romain Playground, but it had never occurred to him that he too might become a musician. That afternoon Fausto knew his mission in life: to play guitar in his own band; to sweat out his songs and prance around the stage; to make money and dress weird.

Fausto turned off the television set and walked outside, wondering how he could get enough money to buy a guitar. He couldn't ask his parents because they would just say, "Money doesn't grow on trees" or "What do you think we are, bankers?" And besides, they hated rock music. They were into the *conjunto* music[1] of Lydia Mendoza, Flaco Jimenez, and Little Joe and La Familia. And, as Fausto recalled, the last album they bought was *The Chipmunks Sing Christmas Favorites*.

But what the heck, he'd give it a try. He returned inside and watched his mother make tortillas. He leaned against the kitchen counter, trying to work up the nerve to ask her for a guitar. Finally, he couldn't hold back any longer.

"Mom," he said, "I want a guitar for Christmas."

She looked up from rolling tortillas. "Honey, a guitar costs a lot of money."

"How 'bout for my birthday next year," he tried again.

"I can't promise," she said, turning back to her tortillas, "but we'll see."

Fausto walked back outside with a buttered tortilla. He knew his mother was right. His father was a warehouseman at Berven Rugs, where he made good money but not enough to buy everything his children wanted. Fausto decided to mow lawns to earn money, and was pushing the mower down the street before he realized it was winter and no one would hire him. He returned the mower and picked up a rake. He hopped onto his sister's bike (his had two flat tires) and rode north to the nicer section of Fresno in search of work. He went door-to-door, but after three hours he managed to get only one job, and not to rake leaves. He

---

1. *conjunto* (kōn hōōn′ tō) **music:** Music of the Mexican American border.

was asked to hurry down to the store to buy a loaf of bread, for which he received a grimy, dirt-caked quarter.

He also got an orange, which he ate sitting at the curb. While he was eating, a dog walked up and sniffed his leg. Fausto pushed him away and threw an orange peel skyward. The dog caught it and ate it in one gulp. The dog looked at Fausto and wagged his tail for more. Fausto tossed him a slice of orange, and the dog snapped it up and licked his lips.

"How come you like oranges, dog?"

The dog blinked a pair of sad eyes and whined.

"What's the matter? Cat got your tongue?" Fausto laughed at his joke and offered the dog another slice.

At that moment a dim light came on inside Fausto's head. He saw that it was sort of a fancy dog, a terrier or something, with dog tags and a shiny collar. And it looked well fed and healthy. In his neighborhood, the dogs were never licensed, and if they got sick they were placed near the water heater until they got well.

This dog looked like he belonged to rich people. Fausto cleaned his juice-sticky hands on his pants and got to his feet. The light in his head grew brighter. It just might work. He called the dog, patted its muscular back, and bent down to check the license.

"Great," he said. "There's an address."

The dog's name was Roger, which struck Fausto as weird because he'd never heard of a dog with a human name. Dogs should have names like Bomber, Freckles, Queenie, Killer, and Zero.

Fausto planned to take the dog home and collect a reward. He would say he had found Roger near the freeway. That would scare the daylights out of the owners, who would be so happy that they would probably give him a reward. He felt bad about lying, but the dog *was* loose. And it might even really be lost, because the address was six blocks away.

Fausto stashed the rake and his sister's bike behind a bush, and, tossing an orange peel every time Roger became distracted, walked the dog to his house. He hesitated on the porch until Roger began to scratch the door with a muddy paw. Fausto had come this far, so he figured he might as well go through with it. He knocked softly. When no one answered, he rang the doorbell. A man in a silky bathrobe and slippers opened the door and seemed confused by the sight of his dog and the boy.

"Sir," Fausto said, gripping Roger by the collar. "I found your dog by the freeway. His dog license says he lives here." Fausto looked down at the dog, then up to the man. "He does, doesn't he?"

The man stared at Fausto a long time before saying in a pleas-ant voice, "That's right." He pulled his robe tighter around him because of the cold and asked Fausto to come in. "So he was by the freeway?"

"Uh—huh."

"You bad, snoopy dog," said the man, wagging his finger. "You probably knocked over some trash cans, too, didn't you?"

Fausto didn't say anything. He looked around, amazed by this house with its shiny furniture and a television as large as the front window at home. Warm bread smells filled the air and music full of soft tinkling floated in from another room.

"Helen," the man called to the kitchen. "We have a visitor." His wife came into the living room wiping her hands on a dish towel and smiling. "And who have we here?" she asked in one of the softest voices Fausto had ever heard.

"This young man said he found Roger near the freeway."

Fausto repeated his story to her while staring at a perpetual clock with a bell-shaped glass, the kind his aunt got when she celebrated her twenty-fifth anniversary. The lady frowned and said, wagging a finger at Roger, "Oh, you're a bad boy."

"It was very nice of you to bring Roger home," the man said. "Where do you live?"

"By that vacant lot on Olive," he said. "You know, by Brownie's Flower Place."

The wife looked at her husband, then Fausto. Her eyes twinkled triangles of light as she said, "Well, young man, you're probably hungry. How about a turnover?"

"What do I have to turn over?" Fausto asked, thinking she was talking about yard work or something like turning trays of dried raisins.

"No, no, dear, it's a pastry." She took him by the elbow and guided him to a kitchen that sparkled with copper pans and bright yellow wallpaper. She guided him to the kitchen table and gave him a tall glass of milk and something that looked like an *empanada*.[2] Steamy waves of heat escaped when he tore it in two. He ate with both eyes on the man and woman who stood arm-in-arm smiling at him. They were strange, he thought. But nice.

"That was good," he said after he finished the turnover. "Did you make it, ma'am?"

"Yes, I did. Would you like another?"

"No, thank you. I have to go home now."

As Fausto walked to the door, the man opened his wallet and took out a bill. "This is for you," he said. "Roger is special to us, almost like a son."

Fausto looked at the bill and knew he was in trouble. Not with these nice folks or with his parents but with himself. How could

---

2. *empanada* (em´ pä nä´ dä): Mexican pastry, often filled with meat.

he have been so deceitful?[3] The dog wasn't lost. It was just having a fun Saturday walking around.

"I can't take that."

"You have to. You deserve it, believe me," the man said.

"No, I don't."

"Now don't be silly," said the lady. She took the bill from her husband and stuffed it into Fausto's shirt pocket. "You're a lovely child. Your parents are lucky to have you. Be good. And come see us again, please."

Fausto went out, and the lady closed the door. Fausto clutched the bill through his shirt pocket. He felt like ringing the doorbell and begging them to please take the money back, but he knew they would refuse. He hurried away, and at the end of the block, pulled the bill from his shirt pocket: It was a crisp twenty-dollar bill.

"Oh, man, I shouldn't have lied," he said under his breath as he started up the street like a zombie. He wanted to run to church for Saturday confession,[4] but it was past four-thirty, when confession stopped.

He returned to the bush where he had hidden the rake and his sister's bike and rode home slowly, not daring to touch the money in his pocket. At home, in the privacy of his room, he examined the twenty-dollar bill. He had never had so much money. It was probably enough to buy a secondhand guitar. But he felt bad, like the time he stole a dollar from the secret fold inside his older brother's wallet.

Fausto went outside and sat on the fence. "Yeah," he said. "I can probably get a guitar for twenty. Maybe at a yard sale—things are cheaper."

His mother called him to dinner.

The next day he dressed for church without anyone telling him. He was going to go to eight o'clock mass.

"I'm going to church, Mom," he said. His mother was in the kitchen cooking *papas*[5] and *chorizo con huevos*.[6] A pile of tortillas lay warm under a dishtowel.

"Oh, I'm so proud of you, Son." She beamed, turning over the crackling *papas*.

His older brother, Lawrence, who was at the table reading the funnies, mimicked, "Oh, I'm so proud of you, my son," under his breath.

At Saint Theresa's he sat near the front. When Father Jerry began by saying that we are all sinners, Fausto thought he

---

3. **deceitful:** Dishonest.
4. **confession:** Religious observance in which one admits his or her sins.
5. ***papas*** (pä´ päs): Potatoes.
6. ***chorizo con huevos*** (chôr e̅´ so̅ kon´ hwä´ vo̅s): Sausage with eggs.

looked right at him. Could he know? Fausto fidgeted with guilt. No, he thought. I only did it yesterday.

Fausto knelt, prayed, and sang. But he couldn't forget the man and the lady, whose names he didn't even know, and the *empanada* they had given him. It had a strange name but tasted really good. He wondered how they got rich. And how that dome clock worked. He had asked his mother once how his aunt's clock worked. She said it just worked, the way the refrigerator works. It just did.

Fausto caught his mind wandering and tried to concentrate on his sins. He said a Hail Mary and sang, and when the wicker basket came his way, he stuck a hand reluctantly in his pocket and pulled out the twenty-dollar bill. He ironed it between his palms, and dropped it into the basket. The grown-ups stared. Here was a kid dropping twenty dollars in the basket while they gave just three or four dollars.

There would be a second collection for Saint Vincent de Paul, the lector announced. The wicker baskets again floated in the pews, and this time the adults around him, given a second chance to show their charity, dug deep into their wallets and purses and dropped in fives and tens. This time Fausto tossed in the grimy quarter.

Fausto felt better after church. He went home and played football in the front yard with his brother and some neighbor kids. He felt cleared of wrongdoing and was so happy that he played one of his best games of football ever. On one play, he tore his good pants, which he knew he shouldn't have been wearing. For a second, while he examined the hole, he wished he hadn't given the twenty dollars away.

Man, I coulda bought me some Levi's, he thought. He pictured his twenty dollars being spent to buy church candles. He pictured a priest buying an armful of flowers with *his* money.

Fausto had to forget about getting a guitar. He spent the next day playing soccer in his good pants, which were now his old pants. But that night during dinner, his mother said she remembered seeing an old bass guitarron[7] the last time she cleaned out her father's garage.

"It's a little dusty," his mom said, serving his favorite enchiladas, "But I think it works. Grandpa says it works."

Fausto's ears perked up. That was the same kind the guy in Los Lobos played. Instead of asking for the guitar, he waited for his mother to offer it to him. And she did, while gathering the dishes from the table.

"No, Mom, I'll do it," he said, hugging her. "I'll do the dishes forever if you want."

---

7. **guitarron** (gē´ tär ōn´): Large, six-string guitar used by Mexican musicians.

It was the happiest day of his life. No, it was the second-happiest day of his life. The happiest was when his grandfather Lupe placed the guitarron, which was nearly as huge as a wash-tub, in his arms. Fausto ran a thumb down the strings, which vibrated in his throat and chest. It sounded beautiful, deep and eerie. A pumpkin smile widened on his face.

"OK, *hijo*,[8] now you put your fingers like this," said his grandfather, smelling of tobacco and aftershave. He took Fausto's fingers and placed them on the strings. Fausto strummed a chord on the guitarron, and the bass resounded in their chests.

The guitarron was more complicated than Fausto imagined. But he was confident that after a few more lessons he could start a band that would someday play on "American Bandstand" for the dancing crowds.

---

8. *hijo* (ē´ hō): Son.

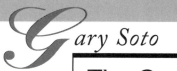

The Gymnast

For three days of my eleventh summer I listened to my mother yap about my cousin, Issac, who was taking gymnastics. She was proud of him, she said one evening at the stove as she pounded a round steak into *carne asada*[1] and crushed a heap of beans into refritos. I was jealous because I had watched my share of "Wide World of Sports" and knew that people admired an athlete who could somersault without hurting himself. I pushed aside my solitary game of Chinese checkers and spent a few minutes rolling around the backyard until I was dizzy and itchy with grass.

That Saturday, I went to Issac's house where I ate plums and sat under an aluminum arbor watching my cousin, dressed in gymnastic shorts and top, do spindly cartwheels and backflips in his backyard while he instructed, "This is the correct way." He breathed in the grassy air, leaped, and came up smiling the straightest teeth in the world.

I followed him to the front lawn. When a car passed, he did a backflip and looked out the side of his eyes to see if any of the passengers were looking. Some pointed while others looked ahead dully at the road.

My cousin was a showoff, but I figured he was allowed the limelight before one appreciative dog who had come over to look. I envied him and his cloth gymnast shoes. I liked the way they looked, slim, black and cool. They seemed special, something I could never slip onto my feet.

I ate the plums and watched him until he was sweaty and out of breath. When he was finished, I begged him to let me wear his cloth shoes. Drops of sweat fell at his feet. He looked at me with disdain, ran a yellow towel across his face, and patted his neck dry. He tore the white tape from his wrists—I liked the tape as well and tried to paste it around my wrists. He washed off his hands. I asked him about the white powder, and he said it kept his hands dry. I asked him why he needed dry hands to do cartwheels and back flips. He said that all gymnasts kept their hands dry, then drank from a bottle of greenish water he said was filled with nutrients.

I asked him again if I could wear his shoes. He slipped them off and said, "OK, just for a while." The shoes were loose, but I liked them. I went to the front yard with my wrists dripping tape

---

1. *carne asada* (cär′ nä ä säd′ ä): Roast meat.

and my hands white as gloves. I smiled slyly and thought I looked neat. But when I did a cartwheel, the shoes flew off, along with the tape, and my cousin yelled and stomped the grass.

I was glad to get home. I was jealous and miserable, but the next day I found a pair of old vinyl slippers in the closet that were sort of like gymnastic shoes. I pushed my feet into them, tugging and wincing because they were too small. I took a few steps, admiring my feet, which looked like bloated water balloons, and went outside to do cartwheels on the front lawn. A friend skidded to a stop on his bike, one cheek fat with sunflower seeds. His mouth churned to a stop. He asked why I was wearing slippers on a hot day. I made a face at him and said that they were gymnastic shoes, not slippers. He watched me do cartwheels for a while, then rode away doing a wheelie.

I returned inside. I looked for tape to wrap my wrists, but could find only circle band-aids in the medicine cabinet. I dipped my hands in flour to keep them dry and went back outside to do cartwheels and, finally, after much hesitation, a backflip that nearly cost me my life when I landed on my head. I crawled to the shade, stars of pain pulsating in my shoulder and neck.

My brother glided by on his bike, smooth as a kite. He stared at me and asked why I was wearing slippers. I didn't answer him. My neck still hurt. He asked about the flour on my hands, and I told him to leave me alone. I turned on the hose and drank cool water.

I walked to Romain playground where I played Chinese checkers and was asked a dozen times why I was wearing slippers. I'm taking gymnastics, I lied, and these are the kind of shoes you wear. When one kid asked why I had white powder on my hands and in my hair, I gave up on Chinese checkers and returned home, my feet throbbing. But before I went inside, I took off the slippers. My toes cooled on the summery grass. I ran a garden hose on my feet and bluish ankles, and a chill ran up my back.

Dinner was a ten-minute affair of piranha-like eating and thirty minutes of washing dishes. Once finished, I returned to the backyard, where I again stuffed my feet into the slippers and did cartwheels by the dizzy dozens. After a while they were easy. I had to move on. I sucked in the summer air, along with the smoke of a faraway barbecue, and tried a backflip. I landed on my neck again, and this time I saw an orange burst behind my eyes. I lay on the grass, tired and sweaty, my feet squeezed in the vise of cruel slippers.

I watched the dusk settle and the first stars, pinpoints of unfortunate light tangled in telephone wires. I ate a plum, cussed, and pictured my cousin, who was probably cartwheeling to the audience of one sleeping dog.

☑ Check Your Comprehension

1. In "The No-Guitar Blues," how does Fausto earn a quarter?

2. Why does Fausto want to earn more money?

3. What lie does Fausto tell when he returns the runaway dog?

4. In "The Gymnast," name two ways in which the narrator tries to be like his cousin Issac.

5. What does the narrator of "The Gymnast" do after he falls on his head for the second time?

◆ Critical Thinking

INTERPRET

1. Fausto gives his reward money to the church. (a) Why do you think he does this? (b) What does this tell you about his personality? **[Infer]**

2. Why is Fausto so happy when his mother offers him the guitarron? **[Draw Conclusions]**

3. Name two reasons that the narrator of "The Gymnast" tries to be like his cousin. **[Support]**

COMPARE LITERARY WORKS

4. Which character do you think is more likely to achieve his goals? In other words, will Fausto become a talented guitar player, or will the narrator become an expert gymnast? Explain your answer. **[Evaluate]**

APPLY

5. Fausto and the narrator of "The Gymnast" are determined to achieve their goals. Name one goal you are determined to achieve, and explain how you plan to achieve it. **[Relate]**

Gary Soto

Ballet folklórico

My friends
Know me
As the girl
In jeans
5   And tennis shoes
Flecked with mud.
My neighbor
Knows me
As the one
10   Who left skid marks
On the sidewalk
And a little spot
Of blood
From my left knee.
15   And my teacher
Knows me as
The second-best speller
Against the boys on
The other side
20   Of the classroom,
Boys with fingers
In their mouths,
Falling like bowling pins.
But on Saturday,
25   Not everyone knows
I take *ballet folklórico*,[1]
My feet squeezed
Into shoes,
My smile caught
30   In the mirrors
On the wall,
And my cheeks hot
As the inside of a glove.
I love dancing,
35   And the ring
Of our steps
On the wooden floor.

---

1. **ballet folklórico** (ba lā´ fōlk lôr´ ē kō): Mexican folk dancing.

I love my dress,
Flushed with the colors
40 Of México,
Twirling like an umbrella.
It's joy,
And swing of
Bodies, elbow
45 To elbow, dip
And swing, slap
And click of boots.
When I practice,
My hair unrolls
50 From its bun,
And with a bobby pin
In my mouth,
I fix it back.
I can dance
55 The *jarabe tapatío*,[2]
The quick steps of
las danzas de los listones,[3]
Three different *Huapangos*,[4]
Jaranas,[5] and *sones de Veracruz*,[6]
60 The *jarocho*[7] with
My *guapo*[8] cousin, Isaac.
If called on, I can dance
My favorite, *Los viejitos*,[9]
"Dance of the Little Old Men."

65 Once, at a school carnival,
I danced "The Little Old Men."
My *abuelo*[10] was there,
Leaning on his cane,
Eyes bright,
70 His face shiny
As a moon
Over a hill.

---

2. *jarabe tapatío* (hä rä´ bā tä pä tē´ ō): A Mexican tapping dance.
3. *las danzas de los listones* (läs dän´ säs dā lōs lēs tōn´ ās): "Dances of the ribbons," similar to a May dance with ribbons tied to a pole.
4. *Huapangos* (hwä pän´ gōs): A dance whose name comes from the Nahuatl language and means "dance over a wooden platform."
5. *Jaranas* (hä rän´ äs): Strumming guitars.
6. *sones de Veracruz* (sōn´ ās dā ve´ rä crōōs´): Songs of Veracruz.
7. *jarocho* (hä rō´ chō): The most rhythmically complex of the *sones de Veracruz*.
8. *guapo* (gwä´ pō): Good-looking, cute.
9. *Los viejitos* (los vē e he´ tōs): Dance of the little old men; a folk dance from the Michoacán region of Mexico.
10. *abuelo* (ä bwā´ lō): Grandfather.

I danced behind
A mask of a *viejo*,[11]
75 My steps staggering
And drunken.
I swayed
And fell, got to
One knee, and fell again,
80 Then tripped
Over my heels.
My dance steps
Were rickety
As a porch,
85 Lopsided
As a three-legged table.
I tapped my cane
And staggered,
Me, the girl
90 Playing a *viejo*
To laughter
And applause.
When the dance finished,
We ripped off
95 Our masks, bowed,
And shuffled away.
Later, my *abuelo*
Came up to me,
Tapping his cane,
100 One shoelace undone.
"I used to do that *danza*,"[12]
My *abuelo* told me.
"You did?" I asked.
"Yes," he answered,
105 "And, *pues*,[13] I got good at it."
He winked at me
And staggered away,
Knees buckling,
Back hunched,
110 And his cane
Dancing on the blacktop.

---

11. *viejo* (vē ā´ hō): Old man.
12. *danza* (dän´ sä): Dance.
13. *pues* (pwās): Well.

*G*ary Soto

Ode to Pomegranates

Just as fall
Turns the air,
And the first
Leaves begin
5   To parachute
To the ground,
The pomegranate[1]
Bursts a seam
And the jewels
10   Wink a red message.
The García brothers
Have been waiting.
All summer
They have lived
15   On candies and plums,
Bunches of grapes
From their *tío*[2]
In the San Joaquin Valley.
Now it's time
20   On this bright Saturday
When they'll jump
The fence of Mrs. López
And pluck off
Six pomegranates.
25   It's six sins
Against them,
But they just can't help
Themselves. They
Love that treasure
30   Of jewels glistening
Through cracked husks.
Sitting at a curb,
The Garcías bite
Into the pomegranates,
35   And their mouths
Fill with the shattered
Sweetness. The blood
Of the fruit runs

---

1. pomegranate (päm´ ə gran´ it): A tree fruit that ripens in the fall and has bright red juicy seeds that are slightly tart.
2. *tío* (tē´ o): Uncle.

Down to their elbows,
40 Like a vein,
Like a red river,
Like a trail of red ants.
They eat without talking.
When they finish
45 With four of the six
Pomegranates,
Their mouths are red.
As the laughter of clowns.
And they are clowns.
50 Mrs. López has been watching
Them from the windows.
She can see that they
Are boys who live
By the sweet juice on tongues.
55 From her porch,
She winds up
Like a pitcher
And hurls a pomegranate.
It splatters
60 In the road,
A few inches from them,
The juice flying up
Like blood.
They boys run down
55 The street,
With shame smeared
On their dirty faces.

Gary Soto

Pepper Tree

We tapped you into a snug hole,
Staked you to a piece
Of lumber that was once the house,
A rail from the back porch;
5   That, too, was a tree, cut,
Milled, and slapped with wire
For shipment, back in the thirties.
Don't worry. You're not
Going anywhere, hatrack. The wind
10   Comes, the sparrows come —
The rain pointless against
Your branches, notched
With a promise of leaves.
You are here, under rain
15   And the rain of *Get Big,* from my child.

The truth is I don't care
For the street, the banged
Cars and three-legged dogs,
The scuttle of bags
20   Blowing from the grocery, Lucky Day.
I don't care for the billboard,
The wires crossing and recrossing.
From the front window
I want to look at you,
25   Green and moving like the sea
In wind. I want you to grow
Heavy with sparrows, and if
A gull has an off day
In the weary sky, let
30   Your branches bear its screams,
The scraping beak. Let its wings
Open on sores, shoulders hunch,
And eyes stare me back to church.
Under this weight, that color,
35   Stand up, bend a little, be here tomorrow.

☑ Check Your Comprehension

1. Describe how the speaker dresses for her *ballet folklórico* lessons.
2. Describe how she performs the "Dance of the Little Old Men."
3. What do the García brothers do in "Ode to Pomegranates"?
4. What does Mrs. López do when she sees the boys eating?
5. What does the speaker in "Pepper Tree" hope the pepper tree will grow to cover?

◆ Critical Thinking

INTERPRET

1. At the end of "Ballet folklórico," the grandfather says that he "got good at" the "Dance of the Little Old Men." What does he mean? **[Analyze]**
2. How does the speaker in "Ode to Pomegranates" feel about the boys' misbehavior? How does Mrs. López feel about it? Use details from the poem to support your answers. **[Distinguish]**
3. Why does the speaker in "Pepper Tree" plant the tree? **[Interpret]**

COMPARE LITERARY WORKS

4. In much of his work, Gary Soto celebrates his neighborhood. Do you see evidence of this in any of these poems? Support your answer with details from the poems. **[Connect]**

APPLY

5. Many of Soto's poems are about everyday activities, like taking dance lessons or planting a tree. Why do you think he writes about these ordinary things? **[Speculate]**

Gary Soto

Comparing and Connecting the Author's Works

◆ Literary Focus: Characters' Motives

Characters' motives are the reasons for their actions. Creating characters with realistic motives helps readers to identify with and believe in them.

Sometimes, a writer directly states a character's motive. For example, Soto writes that Fausto wanted to earn money in order to buy a guitar. More often, though, a writer will provide clues, and the reader must determine on his or her own why a character acts in a certain way.

To understand characters' motives, ask yourself "why" questions about their actions. This chart shows some of the questions you might ask as you think about Fausto's motives.

Action	Motive
Why does Fausto want to earn money?	He wants to buy a guitar.
Why does Fausto lie about where he found Roger?	He thinks the highway story will scare the dog's owners into giving him a big reward.
Why does Fausto give up the reward money?	He feels guilty for lying.

1. Why does the speaker in "Ballet folkórico" cherish her dance lessons?
2. Why do the boys take the fruit from Mrs. López in "Ode to Pomegranates"?
3. Why does Mrs. López refrain from punishing the boys?
4. Why does the speaker in "Pepper Tree" want the tree to grow sturdy and large?

◆ Drawing Conclusions About Gary Soto's Work

Gary Soto says that "Even though I write a lot about life in the barrio, I am really writing about the feelings and experiences of most American kids." In other words, he hopes that young readers of all backgrounds, not just Mexican Americans or people who grew up in a barrio, can relate to his work.

Use a chart like the one below to evaluate which character in his stories or poems you relate to most. After you fill in the chart, write a paragraph about the character and why you identify with him or her.

Character	Description	Why I Can Relate
Fausto	Makes a mistake but learns from it	I once had a similar experience when I didn't study for a test . . .

◆ Idea Bank

Writing

1. **Reader's Report** Write a review in which you recommend one of Soto's stories or poems. Tell what you think are the strengths of the writing and what kinds of readers will enjoy it. Try to make readers curious to read it for themselves.
2. **Short Story** Write a short story based on one of Gary Soto's poems. You might choose to retell the story of the poem in prose, or to tell a different story using the same character. Reread the poem to review details

about the characters and events before you begin writing.

3. **Respond to Criticism** Reviewer Caroline S. McKinney has praised Soto's stories, saying that each one is "a little treasure of human experience skillfully drawn with poetic sensitivity." What do you think she means? Write a paragraph explaining the quote and telling whether you agree with it. Use examples from "The No-Guitar Blues" and "The Gymnast" to support your opinion.

Speaking, Listening, and Viewing

4. **Oral Interpretation** Rehearse an oral interpretation of one of Gary Soto's poems. Read the poem slowly and clearly, emphasizing the words and ideas you think are most important. Share your presentation with a small audience of friends, classmates, or family members. **[Performing Arts Link]**

5. **Interview** Imagine that Gary Soto is coming to visit your class. With a partner, write a list of ten questions you want to ask about his life, writing process, or work. If possible, do research in the library or on the Internet to find the answers.

Researching and Representing

6. **Multimedia Presentation** With a small group, create a multimedia presentation on one aspect of Mexican American culture. Look for an idea in one of Soto's selections. For example, you might find out more about the folk dances described in "Ballet folklórico" or about growing up in a barrio. Present your work to your class. **[Social Studies Link; Group Activity]**

◆ Further Reading, Listening, and Viewing

- *Taking Sides* (1991) and *Pacific Crossing* (1992). Two novels tell about the challenges faced by Mexican American eighth-grader Lincoln Mendoza.

- *A Summer Life* (1991). Soto remembers childhood events in this collection of short autobiographical essays.

- *Coming of Age in America: A Multicultural Anthology* by Mary Frosch, forward by Gary Soto (1994). Fifteen writers from diverse backgrounds share stories about growing up.

- *Neighborhood Odes* (1992). Energetic poems bring to life the rhythms of a Mexican American neighborhood.

On the Web:

http://www.phschool.com/atschool/literature
Go to the student edition *Bronze*. Proceed to Unit 1. Then, click Hot Links to find Web sites featuring Gary Soto.

Eve Merriam In Depth

> "I love to fool around with language. The language, really, is like a game. Some people like to bounce balls or jump rope, and I like to skip around and doodle with the sounds of words."
>
> —*Eve Merriam*

EVE MERRIAM felt that poetry was fun, like music and games. It was also food for the heart, the mind, and the soul. She once said that "to be well fed, we need poems along with our daily bread. The poem has juicy, joyful sustenance. Don't save it for special occasions. Take that magical fruit right this minute and then share it."

A Passion for Words

Eve Merriam was born on July 19, 1916, in Philadelphia, Pennsylvania, the youngest of four children. Her parents owned a chain of dress shops, which inspired her lifelong interest in fashion.

Even as a child, Merriam's true passions were words and music. From an early age, she loved reading poems that were funny or that told a story. She also loved going to musicals, especially those by Gilbert and Sullivan, which were full of tongue-twisting verses. One of her favorite books as a child was *Alice's Adventures in Wonderland,* a book that fed her fascination with nonsense verse and word play. Merriam was a tap dancer, too, and she credited her love of the rhythms of language to her dancing experiences.

As a teenager, Merriam began writing poems for the school newspaper. At that time, she never dreamed of actually becoming a professional writer. She simply wrote poems because she needed to. As she once explained, "I think one is chosen to be a poet. You write poems because you *must* write them; because you can't live your life without writing them."

Years in Journalism

After graduating from college in the 1930's, Merriam took a job as a copywriter at an advertising agency and later at the Columbia Broadcasting System (CBS), where she wrote radio documentaries and scripts in verse. She also had her own radio show on modern poetry from 1942–1946. In 1947 she became a fashion copy editor at *Glamour* magazine.

All the while, Merriam continued writing poetry, and in 1946, she won the Yale Younger Poets Prize for her first volume of poetry, *Family Circle.* She was thrilled that the contest judge who chose her book for the award was the poet Archibald MacLeish, one of her personal heros.

Kidding Around

It wasn't until 1962, when she was in her forties, that Merriam published her first book of poems for children, *There Is No Rhyme for Silver.* The book contains fifty-one poems that celebrate the joy of playing around with the sounds of words, especially with rhymes. Two similar books of poetry soon followed: *It Doesn't Always Have to Rhyme* (1964) and *Catch a Little Rhyme* (1966).

Getting Serious

Although Merriam celebrated the simple joys of everyday life in many of her poems, she also had a strong social conscience, and much of her work deals with serious social issues such as feminism, racial equality, saving the environment, and protesting the evils of war. Merriam wrote poetry and nonfiction books on these issues for both children and adults. Among these books is *Independent Voices,* a collection of poems about Americans past and present whom Merriam admired, including Elizabeth Blackwell, the first woman doctor in the United States, and African American leader Frederick Douglass.

Merriam was also an accomplished playwright. During the 1970's, she wrote the Obie Award-winning play *The Club,* a satire of men-only clubs that existed at the turn of the twentieth century. Other plays she wrote in this period include *Out of Our Father's House* (1975), *At Her Age* (1979), and *And I Ain't Finished Yet* (1982).

National Recognition In 1981 Merriam won the National Council of Teachers of English Award for Excellence in Poetry for Children for the entire body of her work. She became a popular speaker and adviser in the teaching of poetry, and she gave many readings and workshops for students.

As always, Merriam continued to write poetry. Among the volumes she published in the 1980's are *Jamboree: Rhymes for All Times, Blackberry Ink, A sky Full of Poems,* and *Fresh Paint.* Merriam died of cancer on April 11, 1992, at the age of seventy-five.

◆ The Mind of a Poet

In many of her poems, Eve Merriam explores how the mind of a poet works: how the poet gathers impressions of the world through the five senses, saves those impressions as images in the brain, and then converts the images into words.

Scientists are only just beginning to understand the mysterious processes by which the brain is able to carry out this complex action known as creativity. They do know that all higher brain functions occur in the cerebral cortex, the crinkled outer surface of the brain, and that there are separate areas in the cortex for interpreting different types of sensory input: sights, sounds, smells, touches, and tastes. They also know that there are separate pathways that allow the brain to link, or associate different types of impressions and turn them into images and words.

With the introduction of magnetic resonance imaging, or MRI, scientists can now study which parts of the brain are used when people perform different types of thinking. No matter how much the scientists learn, however, the magical mind of a poet will probably always remain somewhat of a mystery.

◆ Literary Works

Poetry
- *There Is No Rhyme for Silver* (1962)
- *It Doesn't Always Have to Rhyme* (1964)
- *Catch a Little Rhyme* (1966)
- *Independent Voices* (1968)
- *I Am a Man: Ode to Martin Luther King, Jr.* (1971)
- *Boys and Girls, Girls and Boys* (1972)
- *Out Loud* (1973)
- *A Husband's Notes About Her: Fictions* (1976)
- *Jamboree: Rhymes for All Times* (1984)
- *Blackberry Ink: Poems* (1985)
- *A Sky Full of Poems* (1986)
- *Fresh Paint: New Poems* (1986)
- *Chortles: New and Selected Wordplay Poems* (1989)
- *The Singing Green: New and Selected Poems for All Seasons* (1992)

Nonfiction
- *Growing Up Female in America: Ten Lives* (1971)

Plays
- *Out of Our Father's House* (1975)
- *The Club* (1976)
- *At Her Age* (1979)
- *And I Ain't Finished Yet* (1982)

*E*ve Merriam

A New Pencil

The thing is,
you cannot write with it
until the point is sharpened
so turn it round and round

5   too few turnings
and the marks will be faint
too many
and the point will break

so turn and turn and
10   catch the wooden shavings
thin as soap slivers
my immigrant grandmother saved.

"You never know when bad times
are due to come round again;
15   besides, why waste anything?"
and so she saved and savored

the marrow in the meat bone at the bottom of the pot
the wilted tops of celery
chop them and start another simmering stew
20   that way the flame never has to go out

and in her sewing basket
ribbon from gift wrappings, bits of cloth,
lonely buttons, stray pieces of elastic;
what on earth for?

25   "You never know," she shrugs again,
"even with you and your friends growing up,
the world's not perfect yet
and if it needs stretching or holding together,

well, here, here's a pencil,
30   write something about it."

On the First Snowfall

On the first snowfall
there is a pinhole
in the pillow of the sky

a feather
5   from a white dove
is falling from the sky

a petal
from a white rose
is falling from the sky

10   a tiny corner
of a page from a bank book
is falling from the sky

the petal
melts on my mouth
15   the feather
turns into a pen
and I write in the book
the silent word
        snow

20   I write it over and over
I write more words
secret words
scarlet words
greedy words
25   no one will now

the snow will cover my dreams.

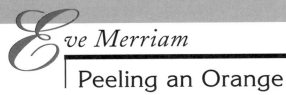

Peeling an Orange

Tearing the skin carelessly
like yesterday's newspaper

or meticulously,[1]
a carpenter restoring the spiral staircase in the castle

5   the juice
a rainspout gurgle

the smell
piercing the fog.

---

1. **meticulously** (mə tik´ yōō ləs lē): Extremely carefully.

☑ Check Your Comprehension

1. In "A New Pencil," what does the grand-mother save? Why does she save these things?
2. To what does Merriam compare snowflakes in "On the First Snowfall"?
3. To what does Merriam compare an orange peel in "Peeling an Orange"?

◆ Critical Thinking

INTERPRET
1. The grandmother in "A New Pencil" "saved and savored" seemingly useless things. How is writing a poem a way of saving and savoring things? **[Connect]**

2. In "On the First Snowfall," what character-istics of snow are appealing to Merriam? **[Infer]**
3. In "Peeling an Orange," why does Merriam wait until the end of the poem to describe the smell of the orange? **[Draw Conclusions]**

COMPARE LITERARY WORKS
4. Both "A New Pencil" and "On the First Snowfall" describe how Merriam uses her experiences as inspiration for her poetry. Find details from both poems that describe how a poet turns experiences into poetry. **[Analyze]**

The Egotistical[1] Orchestra

Vaunts[2] violoncello,
"I'm a fine fellow."

Boasts bass,
"I'm the ace."

5   Flaunts[3] French horn,
"*Sans moi,*[4] all's forlorn."

Pipes flute,
"I'm some sweet toot."

Brags piano, "I'm both upright *and*
10   grand."

Snoots[5] cymbal, "My crashing
is simply smashing."

Vies[6] xylophone,
"I set a high tone."

15   Raps baton, "Come on,
knock off the cacophony,[7]
get Bach to Tchaikovsky,
I'll call the tune."

---

1. **egotistical** (ē gō tis´ ti kəl): Conceited.
2. **vaunts:** Boasts, brags.
3. **flaunts:** Shows off.
4. ***sans moi*** (san mwä): Without me.
5. **snoots:** Says snobbishly or conceitedly.
6. **vies:** Competes; strives to outdo others.
7. **cacophony** (kə käf´ ə nē): Discord; harsh, clashing sounds.

Eve Merriam

Portmanteaux

Two separate words
sometimes condense
into a sound
that's more intense:
5   pairings like those
are *portmanteaux.*[1]

Thus smoke and fog
roll in as *smog,*
breakfast and lunch
10   are served for *brunch,*
scatter and hurry blur into *scurry,*
rush and hustle run into *rustle,*
chuckle and snort cavort as *chortle:*
so language like
15   a giraffe's neck grows.

A turtle that's short
may turn to *tortle,*
a grape and a berry be a *grerry,*
a nest in a nut tree form a *nustle:*

20   so coin[2] new words
and spend and lend
as syllables wander, waft and wend
and blend and bend and never end.

---

1. portmanteaux (pôrt man´ tō): Traveling cases or bags; suitcases.
2. coin: To invent.

☑ Check Your Comprehension

1. Summarize in a few words what all the instruments in "The Egotistical Orchestra" are saying.

2. How does the baton in "The Egotistical Orchestra" put an end to the instruments' discussion?

3. In "Portmanteaux," why are the words *smog, brunch,* and *chortle* all examples of portmanteaux words?

4. At the end of "Portmanteaux," what does Merriam encourage her readers to do?

◆ Critical Thinking

INTERPRET

1. A pun is a joke that plays on words that have double meanings. Explain the puns used by piano, cymbal, xylophone, and baton in "The Egotistical Orchestra." **[Analyze; Interpret]**

2. Explain the pun in the following lines from "Portmanteaux": "so coin new words/and spend and lend." **[Interpret]**

3. Why do you think Merriam enjoys sharing puns with readers? **[Draw Conclusions]**

APPLY

4. In "Portmanteaux," Merriam invents three of her own portmanteaux words: *tortle, grerry,* and *nustle.* Make up your own portmanteaux word and explain what two words it comes from. **[Apply]**

COMPARE LITERARY WORKS

5. In both "The Egotistical Orchestra" and "Portmanteaux," Merriam shows the fun of playing with the sounds and meanings of words. Which poem do you think is more fun to read? Use details from the poem to support your choice. **[Evaluate]**

$\mathscr{E}$ve Merriam

Rummage

My mind is a catch-all
of notions, ideas, sallys,[1] a foray,[2]
scribble a jotting—

like an attic trunk filled with junk:
5   hodgepodge of rag-tag,
worn-out boots, buttons,
torn-pocketed vest, patchwork,
dog-eared stack of postcards, crumpled Christmas
    wrapping
10   twine tinsel tassels tangle snarl all knotted a snag of
ski-pole bathing suit bent hanger dangling
helter-skelter a clutter a scoop up of pell-mell
beads beanbag hatbox wicker basket of higgeldy-
    piggeldy
15   throwcloth float-cushion scatter-rug hammock
    hassock
a jumble a stow
sloven[3] of stash ravel of stickpin grabbag—

Order! Order! straighten out this disarray,
20   start filing, take inventory, build a shelf,
classify, sort, throw away!

And I promise myself I will
on the next rainy vacation day,
but my mind doesn't mind me;
25   saunters off in the rain
and slinks back with more to pack:
driftwood boat, lamp, table,
stone for a doorstop, stone for a paperweight,
and a gull's feather for tracing in sand
30   notions, ideas, and—.

1. **sallys:** Trips; excursions.
2. **foray:** A raid for plunder or treasure.
3. **sloven:** Something or someone untidy, dirty, or careless.

☑ **Check Your Comprehension**

1. According to "Rummage," what is Merriam's mind like?
2. In the second stanza of "Rummage," what words does Merriam use that mean "confusion" or a "mixed-up assortment"?
3. What change occurs in the third stanza of the poem?
4. In the fourth stanza of "Rummage," how does Merriam's mind react to the demand for order?
5. What words from the first stanza of the poem reappear at the end of the poem?

◆ **Critical Thinking**

INTERPRET

1. How is Merriam's mind like an attic trunk? **[Compare]**

2. Why are Merriam's ideas like twine or tinsel? **[Compare]**
3. Why does Merriam stop using commas to separate the individual items listed in the second stanza of the poem? **[Analyze]**
4. Why does Merriam use the word *slink* to describe how her mind brings in new ideas? **[Interpret]**
5. Why are words from the beginning of the poem repeated at the end of the poem? **[Draw Conclusions]**

EVALUATE

6. Do you think that "an attic trunk filled with junk" is a good way to describe a person's mind? Why or why not? **[Make a Judgment]**

ve Merriam

Why I Did Not Reign

I longed to win the spelling bee
And remembered the rule
I had learned in school:

"I before E,
5   Except after C."

Friend, believe me,
No one was going to deceive me.

Fiercely I practiced, the scepter[1] I'd wield,[2]
All others their shields in the field would yield!

10   Alas, before my very eyes
A weird neighbor in a beige veil
Feigning[3] great height and weighty size
Seized the reins and ran off with the prize.

Now I no longer deign[4] to remember that rule.
15   Neither
Any other either.

---

1. scepter (sep´ tər): A staff carried by a king or queen as a sign of royal power.
2. wield: Hold; control.
3. feigning (fān´ ing): Pretending; putting on a false appearance.
4. deign (dān): Think it fit or worthwhile.

A Cliché

is what we all say
when we're too lazy
to find another way

and so we say

5   *warm as toast,*
       quiet as a mouse,
       slow as molasses,
       quick as a wink.

       Think.
10   Is toast the warmest thing you know?
       Think again, it might not be so.
       Think again: it might even be snow!
       Soft as lamb's wool, fleecy snow,
       a lacy shawl of new-fallen snow.

15   Listen to that mouse go
       scuttling and clawing,
       nibbling and pawing.
       A mouse can speak
       if only a squeak.

20   Is a mouse the quietest thing you know?
       Think again, it might not be so.
       Think again: it might be a shadow.
       Quiet as a shadow,
       quiet as growing grass,
25   quiet as a pillow,
       or a looking glass.

       Slow as molasses,
       quick as a wink.
       Before you say so,
30   take time to think.

       Slow as time passes
       when you're sad and alone;
       quick as an hour can go
       happily on your own.

1. In "Why I Did Not Reign," what words in the poem demonstrate the spelling rule that Merriam learned?
2. In "Why I Did Not Reign," what words disprove the spelling rule that Merriam learned?
3. According to the poem "A Cliché," why do people use cliches?
4. In "A Cliché," what comparisons does Merriam suggest as alternatives to the cliché "quiet as a mouse"?

◆ Critical Thinking

INTERPRET

1. In "Why I Did Not Reign," why does a weird neighbor in a beige veil run off with the prize in the spelling bee? **[Analyze]**

2. In your own words, summarize Merriam's conclusion about the value of spelling rules in "Why I Did Not Reign." **[Summarize]**
3. According to "A Cliché," why should people stop and think before using a cliché? **[Draw Conclusions]**

APPLY

4. Do you agree with the conclusion Merriam draws in "Why I Did Not Reign" about the value of spelling rules? Why or why not? **[Defend]**
5. Take one of the cliches from "A Cliché" and write three original comparisons you could use instead of the cliché. **[Apply]**

ve Merriam

Reply to the Question:
"How Can You Become a Poet?"

take the leaf of a tree
trace its exact shape
the outside edges
and inner lines

5   memorize the way it is fastened to the twig
(and how the twig arches from the branch)
how it springs forth in April
how it is panoplied¹ in July

by late August
10   crumple it in your hand
so that you smell its end-of-summer sadness

chew its woody stem

listen to its autumn rattle

watch as it atomizes² in the November air

15   then in winter
when there is no leaf left
        invent one

---

1. panoplied (pan´ ə plēd): Completely and splendidly displayed.
2. atomizes: Breaks down into small particles.

Eve Merriam

Skywriting

1.
Fireworks!
They shower down as verbs,
and come to rest as nouns.

5   Fountain in reverse,
words that delight take flight,
flash like fireworks in the air,
blazon[1] and remain there.

2.
10 Adjectives like leaves
palpitate[2] the trees.
Yearly the seasons must renew
as April's green and singing sound
falls to silent winter ground.

15 A poem shapes the landscape,
holds the singing green.
Leaves that do not die,
planted in the poem sky.

3.
20 Birds write verses in the sky:
swift verbs that fly,
slow nouns in their downy nest.
Wingbeat repeat, repeat
the symmetry[3] of birds, of words.

25 The flight soaring,
the song outpouring.
The flight dying,
the song still flying.

---

1. **blazon** (blā´ zən): Display themselves; adorn with beauty.
2. **palpitate:** Set something trembling, especially with emotion.
3. **symmetry:** Well-balanced arrangement of parts; harmony.

☑ **Check Your Comprehension**

☑ **Check Your Comprehension**

1. In "Reply to the Question," what senses does Merriam encourage readers to use when studying a leaf?
2. According to "Reply to the Question," what should readers do in winter?
3. According to "Skywriting," how are words like fireworks?
4. According to "Skywriting," where can you find "Leaves that do not die"?
5. According to "Skywriting," what do birds and words have in common?

◆ **Critical Thinking**

INTERPRET

1. How are the instructions in "Reply to the Question" related to the process of becoming a poet? **[Connect]**

2. Only the last line of "Reply to the Question" describes the poet actually creating something. Why doesn't Merriam tell more about the actual writing of a poem? **[Analyze]**
3. In "Skywriting," Merriam says that a poem "holds the singing green." What do you think she means? **[Interpret]**
4. Why do you think Merriam compares things in nature to parts of speech such as verbs, nouns, and adjectives? **[Interpret]**

COMPARE LITERARY WORKS

5. According to both "Reply to the Question" and "Skywriting," what connection do poets have with nature? **[Connect]**

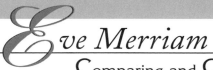
Eve Merriam

Comparing and Connecting the Author's Works

◆ Literary Focus: Figurative Language: Simile and Metaphor

Figurative language is writing or speech that is not meant to be taken literally. Poets use figurative language to state ideas in vivid, imaginative ways. Two types of figurative language are similes and metaphors.

A **simile** is a figure of speech that uses *like* or *as* to make a direct comparison between two unlike ideas. For example, in the poem "Rummage," Eve Merriam says that her mind is "like an attic trunk filled with junk." The comparison helps us think about our minds in a new way. Although a mind and a trunk filled with junk are very different, they also have an important similarity: Both can be crammed full of things that are jumbled together and unorganized.

A **metaphor** is a figure of speech in which something is described as though it were something else. For example, in "On the First Snowfall," Eve Merriam describes a snowflake as though it were "a feather from a white dove."

1. Reread section 1 of "Skywriting." What simile does Merriam use to describe words? What do words have in common with the thing Merriam compares them to?

2. Reread "On the First Snowfall." Find three metaphors that Merriam uses to describe snow. Then choose another type of weather, such as rain or hail. Write three metaphors to describe it. When you finish, share your metaphors with a classmate.

◆ Drawing Conclusions About Merriam's Work

Many critics have praised the humor and playfulness in Eve Merriam's poetry.

One critic explains that Merriam "plays with the sounds of words as much as their meaning." Another says that she "delights in playing with the visual, aural [sound], and intellectual effects of words."

Two humorous poems in which Merriam plays with words are "Why I Did Not Reign" and "The Egotistical Orchestra." Use the chart to compare and contrast the playful aspects of these two poems. Fill in the chart with examples of each type of wordplay. If a poem does not include that type of wordplay, draw an **X** through the box.

	"Why I Did Not Reign"	"The Egotistical Orchestra"
Rhymes		
Repeated Consonant Sounds		
Puns (Based on Word Meanings)		
Puns (Based on Word Spellings)		

After filling in the chart, write an essay comparing and contrasting the playful aspects of the two poems. Which poem would be funnier if it were read aloud? Which poem's humor depends more on readers seeing the words on the page? Why?

◆ Idea Bank

Writing

1. **List of Cliches** Reread the poem "A Cliché." Then write your own list

of cliches. For each cliché, suggest a fresher comparison that conveys the same idea more vividly. To get you started, fill in the following cliches: *as easy as ___, as angry as ___, as busy as ___, as dry as ___, as smart as ___.*

2. **Metaphors for Snow** In "On the First Snowfall," Merriam compares snowflakes to feathers, flower petals, and ripped corners from a blank book. How does snow look and feel to you? Write five original metaphors to describe snow. For example, you might write "the snow is a diamond necklace sparkling on the bare tree."

3. **Additional Stanzas** Write three new stanzas for the poem "The Egotistical Orchestra." Each stanza should name a musical instrument and tell what the instrument might say if it could speak. Use rhymes, repeated consonant sounds, and puns to make each stanza humorous.

Speaking and Listening

4. **Poetry Reading** Choose your favorite poem by Eve Merriam, and read it aloud for a small group. Before you meet with your group, practice reading the poem by yourself so that you can vividly express its rhythms, rhymes, meaning, and humor. **[Performing Arts Link]**

Researching and Representing

5. **Nature Study** Reread the poem "Reply to the Question." Then take Merriam's advice and study the leaf of a houseplant, flower, or tree that you like. Take notes on your observations.

Next, write a description of the leaf, and draw or trace it in detail. Display your work in the classroom. **[Science Link; Art Link]**

6. **Collage** With a partner, reread the poem "Rummage." Then interview your partner to find out what kinds of thoughts and images clutter up his or her brain on a typical day. Draw a picture of your partner's head, and paste in pictures from magazines to show the "hodgepodge of rag-tag" in his or her mind. **[Art Link; Group Activity]**

◆ Further Reading, Listening, and Viewing

- Merriam Eve. *Chortles: New and Selected Wordplay Poems* (1989). This volume includes the poems "The Egotistical Orchestra" and "Portmanteaux," as well as several dozen more of Merriam's humorous poems, including "Whodunnit," "Serendipity," and "Mr. Zoo."

- Merriam, Eve. *Out Loud* (1988). This audiocassette recording is Merriam's adaptation of a book of her poems.

- *Eve Merriam* (1974). This video includes an interview with the poet in which she discusses her life and her poetry and also recites some of her poems.

On the Web:

http://www.phschool.com/atschool/literature Go to the student edition *Bronze*. Proceed to Unit 2. Then, click Hot Links to find Web sites featuring Eve Merriam.

Robert Frost In Depth

"Poetic diction is all wrong. Words must be the ordinary words that we hear about us, to which the imagination must give an iridescence. Then only are words really poetic."

—*Robert Frost*

ROBERT FROST became one of America's most loved poets by finding poetry in the language of everyday speech. His writing often explores the way humans connect with the natural world. By focusing on a single element, such as a fallen nest or a stone wall, Frost reveals connections between daily events and the great themes of life, such as love, loss, and community.

From West to East Frost was born in San Francisco, California, in 1874. When he was eleven, Frost's father died and his family moved to Lawrence, Massachusetts, a growing city that was part of New England's textile industry. After graduating from high school, he attended Dartmouth College, but left before the end of his first semester.

Frost then began a series of careers, including farmer, mill worker, newspaper reporter, and teacher. During his spare time, he wrote poetry. In 1894 he sold a poem, "My Butterfly: An Elegy," to a New York literary journal. He dreamed of one day supporting himself as a writer.

Another Country In 1895, Frost married Elinor White. She and Frost had been the top students in their high school class—they shared the title of valedictorian. Frost attended Harvard University as a special student between 1897 and 1899, but he never graduated.

Frost and his family lived on a chicken farm in Derry, New Hampshire, which he inherited from his grandfather. He spent the next eleven years as a farmer. Unable to get his poems published, Frost decided to make a drastic move. In 1912, he sold the farm and moved his family to England. He planned to use the money from the farm to support himself while he worked on his writing.

In England, Frost befriended several well-known writers, including Ezra Pound, who favorably reviewed his work. Within two years, he published his first two volumes of poetry, *A Boy's Will* (1913) and *North of Boston* (1914).

Return to America With his reputation established, Frost moved back to America in 1915. He purchased a farm in Franconia, New Hampshire, with money from the English and American editions of his books.

Frost soon began to give readings and lectures, and these public performances helped him to overcome his natural shyness. He continued to write, placing poems in literary journals and publishing a third book, *Mountain Interval*, in 1916. In 1924 he received the Pulitzer Prize for his book *New Hampshire*.

In public, Frost liked to present himself as a good-natured, folksy farmer who just happened to be a poet. Yet in private, he was a deep thinker. Those who knew him well acknowledged that he was a more complicated person than the humble farmer he shared with the public.

Acclaim and Popular Appeal Frost went on to write many volumes of poetry and win many awards, including three more Pulitzer Prizes. In 1960, at the invitation of President John F. Kennedy, he became the first poet to read his work at a presidential inauguration.

In addition to his growing calendar of public readings and lectures, Frost also taught at many colleges, including Amherst, the University of Michigan, Harvard, and Dartmouth.

Frost's poems reached a wide audience. He used traditional verse forms and conversational language to paint vivid portraits of the New England landscape and lifestyle. His poems have an appealing simplicity, yet contain many layers of meaning. Many readers are drawn to Frost's work because he finds poetry in events that seem common, even ordinary.

A Writer's Commitment Another important reason for Frost's success is his thorough involvement in what he writes. He places himself deep inside his poems and shares his emotional world. He once described his goal of passionate honesty by giving this advice to other writers: "No tears in the writer, no tears in the reader. No surprise in the writer, no surprise in the reader."

Frost was known as a traditional poet because he favored familiar poetic forms. He did not admire much of the experimental poetry that was written in the twentieth century. In a famous critique of Carl Sandburg, a renowned poet who experimented with free verse, Frost said he'd just as soon play tennis without a net as write free verse.

Still, it is a mistake to view Frost as an entirely conventional poet. He helped to pioneer the use of conversational language in poetry, and his work is filled with complex ideas. Frost clearly achieved what he once claimed to be his life's ambition: to write "a few poems it will be hard to get rid of."

◆ The Landscape of New England

Robert Frost is strongly connected to the landscape of New England, where he spent his youth and much of his adult life. He spent most of his years in New Hampshire, Vermont, and Massachusetts, though New England is also comprised of Rhode Island and Connecticut. Understanding the characteristics of this region can help readers better understand Frost's work.

Many of Frost's poems focus on the rugged landscape of the northeastern United States. New England winters are long, cold, and snowy; summers are shorter but can be extremely hot. Scientists classify the climate of the region as humid and continental.

The New England landscape reflects the changing seasons. The plentiful forests often contain both evergreen and deciduous trees. During autumn, leaves on deciduous trees turn vibrant colors and then fall. Evergreens do not lose their needles, so during the winter, snow-covered pine trees are a familiar sight to New Englanders.

◆ Literary Works

- *A Boy's Will* (1913)
- *North of Boston* (1914)
- *Mountain Interval* (1916)
- *New Hampshire: A Poem With Notes and Grace Notes* (1923)
- *West-Running Brook* (1928)
- *The Lovely Shall Be Choosers* (1929)
- *Collected Poems* (1930)
- *The Lone Striker* (1933)
- *A Further Range* (1936)
- *From Snow to Snow* (1936)
- *A Witness Tree* (1942)
- *Come In, and Other Poems* (1943)
- *A Masque of Reason* (1945)
- *Steeple Bush* (1947)
- *The Road Not Taken: An Introduction to Robert Frost* (1951)
- *Hard Not to be King* (1951)

Robert Frost

On a Tree Fallen Across the Road (To hear us talk)

The tree the tempest[1] with a crash of wood
Throws down in front of us is not to bar
Our passage to our journey's end for good,
But just to ask us who we think we are

5   Insisting always on our own way so.
She likes to halt us in our runner tracks,
And make us get down in a foot of snow
Debating what to do without an ax.

And yet she knows obstruction[2] is in vain:
10   We will not be put off the final goal
We have it hidden in us to attain,
Not though we have to seize earth by the pole

And, tired of aimless circling in one place,
Steer straight off after something into space.

---

1. tempest: Storm.
2. obstruction: Blocking.

An Encounter

Once on the kind of day called 'weather breeder,'
When the heat slowly hazes and the sun
By its own power seems to be undone,
I was half boring[1] through, half climbing through
5   A swamp of cedar. Choked with oil of cedar
And scurf[2] of plants, and weary and over-heated,
And sorry I ever left the road I knew,
I paused and rested on a sort of hook
That had me by the coat as good as seated,
10   And since there was no other way to look,
Looked up toward heaven, and there against the blue,
Stood over me a resurrected[3] tree,
A tree that had been down and raised again—
A barkless specter.[4] He had halted too,
15   As if for fear of treading upon me.
I saw the strange position of his hands—
Up at his shoulders, dragging yellow strands
Of wire with something in it from men to men.
"You here?" I said. "Where aren't you nowadays?
20   And what's the news you carry—if you know?
And tell me where you're off for—Montreal?
Me? I'm not off for anywhere at all.
Sometimes I wander out of beaten ways
Half looking for the orchid Calypso."[5]

---

1. boring: Drilling, tunneling.
2. scurf: Scaly covering on some plant parts.
3. resurrected: Brought back to life.
4. specter: Ghost.
5. orchid Calypso (ôr´ kid cə lip´ sō): A delicate pink North American wild-flower found in forest undergrowth.

Robert Frost

The Exposed Nest

You were forever finding some new play.
So when I saw you down on hands and knees
In the meadow, busy with the new-cut hay,
Trying, I thought, to set it up on end,
5   I went to show you how to make it stay,
If that was your idea, against the breeze,
And, if you asked me, even help pretend
To make it root again and grow afresh.
But 'twas no make-believe with you today,
10   Nor was the grass itself your real concern,
Though I found your hand full of wilted fern,
Steel-bright June-grass, and blackening heads of clover.
'Twas a nest full of young birds on the ground
The cutter-bar[1] had just gone champing[2] over
15   (Miraculously without tasting flesh)
And left defenseless to the heat and light.
You wanted to restore them to their right
Of something interposed[3] between their sight
And too much world at once—could means be found
20   The way the nest-full every time we stirred
Stood up to us as to a mother-bird
Whose coming home has been too long deferred,
Made me ask would the mother-bird return
And care for them in such a change of scene
25   And might our meddling make her more afraid.
That was a thing we could not wait to learn.
We saw the risk we took in doing good,
But dared not spare to do the best we could
Though harm should come of it; so built the screen
30   You had begun, and gave them back their shade.
All this to prove we cared. Why is there then
No more to tell? We turned to other things.
I haven't any memory—have you?—
Of ever coming to the place again
35   To see if the birds lived the first night through,
And so at last to learn to use their wings.

---

1. **cutter-bar:** Cutting blade of a hay mower.
2. **champing:** Biting.
3. **interposed:** Placed between.

Hyla Brook

By June our brook's run out of song and speed.
Sought for much after that, it will be found
Either to have gone groping underground
(And taken with it all the Hyla[1] breed
5   That shouted in the mist a month ago,
Like ghost of sleigh-bells in a ghost of snow)—
Or flourished[2] and come up in jewel-weed,
Weak foliage[3] that is blown upon and bent
Even against the way its waters went.
10   Its bed is left a faded paper sheet
Of dead leaves stuck together by the heat—
A brook to none but who remember long.
This as it will be seen is other far
Than with brooks taken otherwhere in song.
15   We love the things we love for what they are.

1. Hyla: Tree frogs.
2. flourished (flu´ rishd): Prospered; grew.
3. foliage: Leaves.

Robert Frost

October

O hushed October morning mild,
Thy leaves have ripened to the fall;
Tomorrow's wind, if it be wild,
Should waste them all.
5   The crows above the forest call;
Tomorrow they may form and go.
O hushed October morning mild,
Begin the hours of this day slow.
Make the day seem to us less brief.
10   Hearts not averse¹ to being beguiled,²
Beguile us in the way you know.
Release one leaf at break of day;
At noon release another leaf;
One from our trees, one far away.
15   Retard the sun with gentle mist;
Enchant the land with amethyst.
Slow, slow!
For the grapes' sake, if they were all,
Whose leaves already are burnt with frost,
20   Whose clustered fruit must else be lost—
For the grapes' sake along the wall.

---

1. averse: Opposed.
2. beguiled (bē gīld´): Charmed; enchanted.

☑ Check Your Comprehension

1. In "On a Tree Fallen Across the Road," why does the tree fall?
2. In "An Encounter," what is the speaker doing? What kind of day is it?
3. What does the speaker decide to do with the nest in "The Exposed Nest"?
4. What happens to the brook in "Hyla Brook" in June?
5. In "October," why does the speaker want October to pass very slowly?

◆ Critical Thinking

INTERPRET

1. In "On a Tree Fallen Across the Road," what does the speaker mean when he says the tree asks passersby "who we think we are"? **[Interpret]**
2. What is the "resurrected tree" in "An Encounter"? Give two details that support your answer. **[Infer]**
3. Identify the element of nature on which Frost focuses in each poem. **[Identify]**
4. Why do you think the speaker in "The Exposed Nest" has no memory of returning to "see if the birds lived the first night through"? **[Speculate]**

COMPARE LITERARY WORKS

5. In what way do "Hyla Brook" and "October" both address the idea of nature's cycles? **[Interpret; Compare]**

Mending Wall

Something there is that doesn't love a wall,
That sends the frozen-ground-swell under it,
And spills the upper boulders in the sun;
And makes gaps even two can pass abreast.[1]
5   The work of hunters is another thing:
I have come after them and made repair
Where they have left not one stone on a stone,
But they would have the rabbit out of hiding,
To please the yelping dogs. The gaps I mean,
10   No one has seen them made or heard them made,
But at spring mending-time we find them there.
I let my neighbor know beyond the hill;
And on a day we meet to walk the line
And set the wall between us once again.
15   We keep the wall between us as we go.
To each the boulders that have fallen to each.
And some are loaves and some so nearly balls
We have to use a spell to make them balance:
"Stay where you are until our backs are turned!"
20   We wear our fingers rough with handling them.
Oh, just another kind of outdoor game,
One on a side. It comes to little more:
There where it is we do not need the wall:
He is all pine and I am apple orchard.
25   My apple trees will never get across
And eat the cones under his pines, I tell him.
He only says, "Good fences make good neighbors."
Spring is the mischief in me, and I wonder
If I could put a notion in his head:
30   "*Why* do they make good neighbors? Isn't it
Where there are cows? But here there are no cows.
Before I built a wall I'd ask to know
What I was walling in or walling out,
And to whom I was like to give offense.
35   Something there is that doesn't love a wall,

---

1. abreast: Side by side.

That wants it down." I could say "Elves" to him,
But it's not elves exactly, and I'd rather
He said it for himself. I see him there
Bringing a stone grasped firmly by the top
40   In each hand, like an old-stone savage armed.
He moves in darkness as it seems to me,
Not of woods only and the shade of trees.
He will not go behind his father's saying,
And he likes having thought of it so well
45   He says again, "Good fences make good neighbors."

Meeting and Passing

As I went down the hill along the wall
There was a gate I had leaned at for the view
And had just turned from when I first saw you
As you came up the hill. We met. But all
5   We did that day was mingle great and small
Footprints in summer dust as if we drew
The figure of our being less than two
But more than one as yet. Your parasol[1]
Pointed the decimal off with one deep thrust.
10   And all the time we talked you seemed to see
Something down there to smile at in the dust.
(Oh, it was without prejudice to me!)
Afterward I went past what you had passed
Before we met and you what I had passed.

---

1. parasol: A lightweight umbrella often carried as sunshade.

Good Hours

I had for my winter evening walk—
No one at all with whom to talk,
But I had the cottages in a row
Up to their shining eyes in snow.

5   And I thought I had the folk within:
I had the sound of a violin;
I had a glimpse through curtain laces
Of youthful forms and youthful faces.

I had such company outward bound.
10   I went till there were no cottages found.
I turned and repented, but coming back
I saw no window but that was black.

Over the snow my creaking feet
Disturbed the slumbering village street
15   Like profanation,[1] by your leave,
At ten o'clock of a winter eve.

---

1. profanation: Destruction of what is holy.

☑ **Check Your Comprehension**

1. In "Mending Wall," what chore are the speaker and his neighbor doing?
2. What event does the poet describe in "Meeting and Passing"?
3. Who keeps the speaker company during his walk in "Good Hours"?

◆ **Critical Thinking**

INTERPRET

1. (a) In "Mending Wall," what suggestion does the speaker consider making to his neighbor? (b) Why doesn't he make this suggestion? **[Interpret]**
2. In "Meeting and Passing," do you think the speaker and the woman will meet again in the future? Support your answer with details from the poem. **[Speculate]**
3. In "Good Hours," what does the speaker mean when he says, "I had such company outward bound"? **[Interpret]**

COMPARE LITERARY WORKS

4. In what ways are the social interactions in "Mending Wall" and "Meeting and Passing" different? **[Compare and Contrast]**

EVALUATE

5. What do you think Frost means by "good fences make good neighbors"? Do you agree with this statement? **[Make a Judgment]**

John F. Kennedy to Robert Frost

After his Cabinet appointment, Udall[1] suggested to President-elect Kennedy that he should try to persuade RF[2] to participate in the inauguration program. Since RF was a poet of the people, the honor would pay tribute to all American literary artists. Udall was immediately authorized to approach RF with the proposal; after RF had informally accepted, Kennedy sent this telegram.

ROBERT FROST   13 DECEMBER 1960
23 [35] BREWSTER ST   WASHINGTON
CAMBRIDGE MASS

I WOULD BE DELIGHTED IF YOU WOULD PARTICIPATE IN THE INAUGURAL CEREMONIES JANUARY TWENTIETH. I KNOW THAT IT WOULD GIVE THE AMERICAN PUBLIC AS MUCH PLEASURE AS IT WOULD MY FAMILY AND ME. THE JOINT CONGRESSIONAL INAUGURAL COMMITTEE WILL SEND YOU A FORMAL INVITATION IN THE NEAR FUTURE. WITH BEST PERSONAL WISHES,

JOHN F. KENNEDY.

---

1. Udall: Stewart L. Udall, Congressman from Arizona and friend of Robert Frost; appointed as Secretary of the Interior in the Cabinet of President John F. Kennedy.
2. RF: Robert Frost

Robert Frost to
John F. Kennedy

PRESIDENT ELECT JOHN F. KENNEDY 14 DECEMBER 1960
WASHINGTON DC   CAMBRIDGE

IF YOU CAN BEAR AT YOUR AGE THE HONOR OF BEING MADE
PRESIDENT OF THE UNITED STATES, I OUGHT TO BE ABLE AT
MY AGE TO BEAR THE HONOR OF TAKING SOME PART IN YOUR
INAUGURATION. I MAY NOT BE EQUAL TO IT BUT I CAN ACCEPT
IT FOR MY CAUSE — THE ARTS, POETRY, NOW FOR THE FIRST
TIME TAKEN INTO THE AFFAIRS OF STATESMEN. I AM GLAD THE
INVITATION PLEASES YOUR FAMILY. IT WILL PLEASE MY FAMILY
TO THE FOURTH GENERATION AND MY FAMILY OF FRIENDS
AND WERE THEY LIVING IT WOULD HAVE PLEASED INORDI-
NATELY THE KIND OF GROVER CLEVELAND DEMOCRATS I HAD
FOR PARENTS.

ROBERT FROST

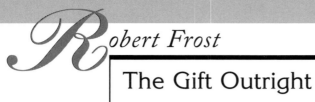

Robert Frost

The Gift Outright

Robert Frost read "The Gift Outright" at the inauguration of President John F. Kennedy. He was the first poet to read at a presidential inauguration.

The land was ours before we were the land's.
She was our land more than a hundred years
Before we were her people. She was ours
In Massachusetts, in Virginia,
But we were England's, still colonials,
Possessing what we still were unpossessed by,
Possessed by what we now no more possessed.
Something we were withholding made us weak
Until we found out that it was ourselves
We were withholding from our land of living,
And forthwith found salvation[1] in surrender.
Such as we were we gave ourselves outright
(The deed of gift was many deeds of war)
To the land vaguely realizing westward,
But still unstoried, artless,[2] unenhanced,
Such as she was, such as she would become.

---

1. salvation: Rescue; being saved from danger, difficulty, or sin.
2. artless: Simple, natural; without artificiality.

☑ Check Your Comprehension

1. What does President Kennedy request in his letter to Robert Frost?
2. How does Frost reply to President Kennedy?
3. In "The Gift Outright," what conflict does the speaker describe?

◆ Critical Thinking

INTERPRET

1. Describe the tone that Frost uses in his reply to Kennedy. Support your answer with at least two details from the letter. **[Analyze]**
2. What does Frost mean when he tells President Kennedy, "I may not be equal to it but I can accept it for my cause—the arts, poetry, now for the first time taken into the affairs of statesmen"? **[Interpret]**
3. In "The Gift Outright," what does the speaker think the American people gained from fighting the Revolution and other wars? **[Interpret]**
4. Kennedy read "The Gift Outright" before his inauguration and enthusiastically agreed with the poem's message. However, he asked Frost to make one change when he read it aloud. Frost agreed. At the inauguration, Frost substituted "will" for "would" in the last line of the poem. Why do you think Kennedy asked for this change? **[Infer]**

EVALUATE

5. Do you think that "The Gift Outright" is an appropriate poem for a presidential inauguration? Why or why not? **[Make a Judgment]**

EXTEND

6. If you could choose one writer to take part in the next presidential inauguration, whom would you choose? Why? **[Literature Link]**

Robert Frost

Some Definitions

"Sometimes I have my doubts of words altogether, and I ask myself what is the place of them. They are worse than nothing unless they do something; unless they amount to deeds, as in ultimatums or battle-cries. They must be flat and final like the show-down in poker, from which there is no appeal. My definition of poetry (if I were forced to give one) would be this: words that have become deeds."

"All poetry is a reproduction of the tones of actual speech."

"There are two types of realists: the one who offers a good deal of dirt with his potato to show that it is a real one, and the one who is satisfied with the potato brushed clean. I'm inclined to be the second kind. To me, the thing that art does for life is to clean it, to strip it to form."

"A poem begins with a lump in the throat; a home-sickness or a love-sickness. It is a reaching-out toward expression; an effort to find fulfilment. A complete poem is one where an emotion has found its thought and the thought has found the words."

from The Unmade Word
or Fetching and Far-Fetching

There are two kinds of language: the spoken language and the written language—our everyday speech which we call the vernacular; and a more literary, sophisticated, artificial, elegant language that belongs to books. We often hear it said that a man talks like a book in this second way. We object to anybody's talking in this literary, artificial English; we don't object to anybody's writing in it; we rather expect people to write in a literary, somewhat artificial style. I, myself, could get along very well without this bookish language altogether. I agree with the poet who visited this country not long ago when he said that all our literature has got to come down, sooner or later, to the talk of everyday life. William Butler Yeats says that all our words, phrases, and idioms[1] to be effective must be in the manner of everyday speech.

We've got to come down to this speech of everyday, to begin with—the hard everyday word of the street, business, trades, work in summer—to begin with; but there is some sort of obligation laid on us, to lift the words of every day, to give them a metaphorical turn. No, you don't want to use that term—give the words a poetic touch. I'll show you what I mean by an example: Take for example the word "lemon," that's a good practical word with no literary associations—a word that you use with the grocer and in the kitchen; it has no literary associations at all; "peach" is another one; but you boys have taken these two words and given them a poetic twist, a poetic movement—you have not left the peach on the tree or in the basket; you couldn't let the lemon alone, you had to move it. What is the need in you of moving words? Take the word "pill" (laughter)—have you let that alone? A person is a pill, a baseball is a pill. You sometimes move even phrases. In baseball you have the phrase, "put one over on him." I suppose I know the origin of that phrase, though it's not one of my invention. Doesn't it mean "pitch one by him that he doesn't hit at at all." Isn't that what it means? Correct me if I'm wrong. "Get his goat" has been explained to me, but I didn't like the explanation. I don't know the origin of that phrase. Now the rest of the world—ladies that never saw a baseball game in their lives, who couldn't trace to their origin any of these phrases—are now using these words and phrases as a matter of everyday

---

1. idioms (id´ ē əmz): Expressions whose meanings differ from the usual syntactic patterns or from the literal meaning of their parts.

speech. Poetry and literature are plumb full, chock full of words and phrases like "lemon, peach, pill, and put one over on him."

But are such expressions allowable in writing? No. When a man sits down with pen and paper to write, he declares his purpose of being original, instead of taking these second-hand words and phrases. I am sick of people who use only these ready-made words and phrases. I like better a boy who invents them for himself—who takes a word or phrase from where it lies and moves it to another place. Did you ever get one up? Are you contented to use the same old words all the time or do you ever get up a new one? Now "fetching" a word or name from its place is what your textbooks call using words figuratively—metaphor, simile, analogy, or allegory[2]—equivalent to using the word "like"; "like a peach"; he isn't a lemon, but "like a lemon." The other day someone said the snow was "mealy." I liked the word. It sounded fresh; but it was an old one that I had heard in the country, and it had lost some of its goodness from use. The other day I heard a new morning salutation; instead of "how d'y'do, how are things coming?"—a new one anyway—a man came into a train and said, "Are you satisfied?" Ever hear that? Is that a going one? At any rate the man had an inspiration and got a new one that pleased me—as if they had had a little quarrel and one wanted to know if the other was satisfied. He had "fetched" the phrase from its regular place to a new and effective place, and got away with it.

He didn't try to be original; but I know people who like that sort of thing so well that they are forever "fetching" words and phrases too far. They overdo it. Well, I don't see why a fellow shouldn't overdo it, at the beginning—it's freshening his language. "How d'y, how do you do, how are you?"—we are tired of those expressions, they need freshening. Now, there are two ways of freshening your language. First by "fetching" words out of their places, and second by going to a thesaurus [a commotion]. You don't know what a thesaurus is? Well, it's a dictionary of synonyms—ministers use 'em, poor men! After they've preached a long time in one place they begin to suspect that their parishioners are getting a little tired of their vocabulary, so they freshen their sermons out of a dictionary. But what I have chiefly in mind is a figurative fetching of fresh words to your use. The word lies in our everyday speech, practical, hard, and unliterary; and that's the way I like the word—there's where my fun with it begins. I don't care for the word already made figurative. I haven't done anything to it. I don't see what more can be done to

---

2. allegory (al´ ə gôr ē): A story in which people, things, and events have symbolic meanings.

it. Mr. Browne doesn't object to my poking a little fun at him. He tells me that yesterday morning, inspired by the brilliant effect of the ice encased trees, reflecting the morning in prismatic[3] colors, he strove to add a new word to your vocabulary by quoting the opening sentence of Emerson's famous Divinity School Address: "In this *refulgent*[4] summer it has been a luxury to draw the breath of life." Of course, anybody would sit up and take notice when a speaker began like that. Undoubtedly there's a freshness there in the use of that word that amounts to brilliance; but you ought not to use the word in just that way. Emerson made it his own; let it alone.

But do the same thing with *your* new words.

---

3. prismatic (priz mat´ ik): Many-colored; brilliant; dazzling.
4. refulgent (ri ful´ gənt): Shining; radiant.

☑ **Check Your Comprehension**

1. In "Some Definitions," name two ways in which Frost defines poetry.
2. In "Some Definitions," according to Frost, what is the purpose of art?
3. Describe the two kinds of language Frost identifies in "The Unmade Word."

◆ **Critical Thinking**

INTERPRET

1. In "Some Definitions," Frost suggests that poetry starts as an emotion. What do you think he means? Can you find an example of this in one of his poems? **[Interpret; Support]**
2. In "The Unmade Word," what is Frost's opinion of using formal language in writing? **[Interpret]**

3. Why doesn't Frost find it acceptable to freshen one's vocabulary simply by using a thesaurus? **[Infer]**

APPLY

4. Choose an overused phrase from daily life, such as "Nice to meet you" or "How are you?" Follow Frost's advice for fetching fresh vocabulary and find a new way to state the same idea. **[Assess; Apply]**

EXTEND

5. Why does Frost think it is so important to use original language when speaking and writing? Do you agree with him? **[Draw Conclusions]**

Robert Frost

Comparing and Connecting the Author's Works

◆ Literary Focus: Figurative Language: Extended Metaphor and Personification

Frost uses everyday language, but he applies many poetic techniques to strengthen the impact of these familiar words. **Figurative language** is language that is not meant to be interpreted literally. The following list describes the two commonly used types of figurative language and gives examples from Frost's poetry.

An **extended metaphor** is a metaphor that continues past a phrase or sentence. (For the definition of a metaphor, see the lesson on Eve Merriam, page 38.)

In "On a Tree Fallen Across the Road," Frost creates an extended metaphor, comparing the fallen tree to a guard blocking a path and asking questions of travelers who want to pass.

Personification is language that gives human traits to nonhuman things.

But I had the cottages in a row
Up to their shining eyes in snow.

In "Good Hours," cottage windows are described as eyes.

1. What kind of figurative language does Frost use in this description of Hyla Brook?

Its bed is left a faded paper sheet
Of dead leaves stuck together by the
heat—

2. Find two examples of personification in "An Encounter."
3. For what is the wall in "Mending Wall" a metaphor?

4. What extended metaphor does Frost refer to in the title "The Gift Outright"?

◆ Drawing Conclusions About Frost's Work

Frost posed as a folksy farmer-poet, and some of his poems seem simple and straightforward. Nonetheless, readers often find deeper meanings when returning to his work, uncovering a sly sense of humor and many wise thoughts about humanity.

Write a paragraph in which you respond to this idea. Choose one of Frost's poems and read it carefully three times. After each reading, jot down some notes in a chart like the one below. In your paragraph, explain how your understanding of the poem changed each time you read it. Did this process help you to better understand the poem? Did it help you to uncover new meanings?

Line	Meaning After First Reading	Meaning After Second Reading	Meaning After Third Reading

◆ Idea Bank

Writing

1. **Summary** Write a one-paragraph summary of Frost's ideas on using original language. Make sure you

answer these questions: What makes language original? Why is it important to use original language? How can one do this?

2. **Personification** Choose five items in your classroom, and describe each one using personification. For example, you might say "The test, for which I hadn't studied, stared up at me in disgust." When you finish, share your descriptions with a partner.

3. **Response Poem** Respond to one of Frost's poems by writing your own poem in a similar form. For example, you might write "November" to respond to "October," or you might imagine what happens after the events described in "The Exposed Nest." Follow Frost's example, using figurative language and everyday speech to help your poem communicate effectively with your audience.

Speaking, Listening, and Viewing

4. **Oral Interpretation** Practice reading one of Frost's poems aloud. If possible, use an audio recorder to play back your rehearsal. Decide which words you will emphasize to make the poem clear to your listeners. Share your reading with the class, your family, or another audience. **[Performing Arts Link]**

5. **Collage** Create a collage to accompany one of Frost's poems. Use illustrations or photographs from magazines, or create your own drawings or paintings. Your collage can include literal elements from the poem, such as a wall or a nest of young birds. It can also include abstract elements, such as related colors and textures. Display your collage and ask viewers to decide which poem the artwork represents. **[Art Link]**

Researching and Representing

6. **Group Presentation** Work with a small group to collect poems from different stages of Frost's life. Put together a short theatrical presentation in which you read selections from the poems and describe events in Frost's life at the time he wrote them. Make sure that each group member is given opportunities to choose and read poems. **[Group Activity]**

7. **Climate Map** Create a set of climate maps for New England. Use the maps to show such features as average winter and summer temperature and precipitation. **[Science Link]**

◆ **Further Reading, Listening, and Viewing**

• Bober, Natalie S., *Restless Spirit: The Story of Robert Frost* (1998). This in-depth biography of the poet's life includes more than twenty of his poems.

• *The Master Poets Collection: Robert Frost—New England in Autumn* (1997). VHS. This documentary explores Frost's life and works.

• *Voices & Visions—Robert Frost* (1988). VHS. This documentary about Frost and his poetry includes several recordings of him reading his own works aloud.

On the Web:

http://www.phschool.com/atschool/literature
Go to the student edition *Bronze*. Proceed to Unit 3. Then, click Hot Links to find Web sites featuring Robert Frost.

James Thurber In Depth

> "In his prose pieces he appears always to have started from the beginning and to have reached the end by way of the middle. It is impossible to read any of the stories from the last line to the first without experiencing a definite sensation of going backward."
>
> — **James Thurber, on himself**

JAMES THURBER was born in Columbus, Ohio, on December 8, 1894. The son of a gentle, worried father and a lively, dramatic mother, James, or "Jamie," as his family called him, was the second of three rambunctious brothers.

Childhood Tragedy One summer afternoon when James was six, he and his brothers were playing a game of William Tell with homemade bows and arrows. James was accidentally shot with an arrow in his left eye, which left him blind in that eye. Unfortunately, an infection spread to his right eye, and by the time Thurber reached middle age, he would be nearly blind.

After his injury, Thurber wasn't able to take part in games and sports. He became a shy, awkward boy who was teased and bullied. Though he was often lonely, he developed a rich imaginative life that would serve him well as a writer.

Thurber blossomed in his high school years and was recognized for his talent in writing and drawing. In his senior year, he was elected class president.

College Years Thurber enrolled at Ohio State University in 1913. He worked on the university's newspaper and humor magazine, and wrote plays and songs for the university's dramatic club. Still, he felt dissatisfied with college life and dropped out in 1918.

The United States was fighting World War I at the time, and many of Thurber's friends were enlisting in the military. Thurber was ineligible for combat duty because of his eye injury, so, instead, he took a job writing codes for the military.

A Budding Journalist Thurber returned home to Columbus in 1920 and worked as a reporter for the Columbus *Dispatch*, where he had his own column. Moving to France in 1925, Thurber got a job at the Paris bureau, and later at the Riviera edition, of the *Chicago Tribune*. In 1926 the writer relocated yet again, this time to New York City, where he was a reporter for the *New York Evening Post*.

A Life-Changing Party In 1927, Thurber met writer E.B. White at a party. White offered to introduce him to Harold Ross, the editor of a struggling new magazine called *The New Yorker*, which specialized in witty, up-to-date humor. After his interview with Ross, Thurber was hired as managing editor of the magazine.

Thurber's style and interests were a perfect fit for *The New Yorker*, and he was a regular contributor to the magazine for the rest of his life, playing an important role in shaping and refining its distinct literary voice. It was also *The New Yorker* that launched Thurber's career as a cartoonist, publishing his quirky but appealing drawings of people and animals.

Literary Success In 1929 Thurber published his first book, followed by two other essay collections, *The Owl in the Attic* (1931) and *The Seal in the Bedroom* (1932). In 1933 came *My Life and Hard Times,* a collection of humorous autobiographical essays, which included "The Night the Bed Fell" and "The Night the Ghost Got In." The book won Thurber instant critical admiration, and many of the essays in it have become classics of American literature. Thurber was now achieving the literary success he had dreamed of, but this period was saddened by a divorce from his first wife in 1935.

A New Beginning Thurber remarried, this time to a magazine editor named Helen Wismer. This marriage lasted for twenty-six years, and his wife eventually became Thurber's business manager, editor, and (as he playfully called her) his "seeing-eye wife." Her love and care helped Thurber through difficult years in which he managed to publish another twenty books of essays and stories, despite his declining eyesight and other health problems. In these years, Thurber also wrote several plays and children's books. Despite being declared legally blind, Thurber continued drawing cartoons, using a device called a Zeiss loupe, a magnifying device like those that jewelers use to examine diamonds.

However, Thurber's eyesight and health continued to deteriorate. In October of 1961 he collapsed after attending a play. Despite surgery, James Thurber died of respiratory failure on November 2, 1961.

◆ The New Yorker

In the 1920's, New York held a special appeal for aspiring writers seeking fame and fortune. Magazines such as *Vanity Fair* and *The Smart Set* were luring bright young men and women to the big city. These writers were creating a new kind of urban humor—modern, witty, sophisticated, and critical. Some of these writers regularly met for lunch at the Algonquin Hotel to discuss the issues of the day and trade humorous quips and insults. Among the members of what was called the Algonquin Roundtable were Dorothy Parker, Robert Benchley, Alexander Woollcott, Ring Lardner, and Harold Ross.

In 1925 Ross decided to start his own magazine to reflect the unique sensibility of New York. Gradually *The New Yorker* began publishing the best of the Algonquin writers, as well as a new crop of humorists and cartoonists that gave the magazine its distinctive flavor. These included James Thurber, E.B. White, S.J. Perelman, Clarence Day, Ogden Nash, Phyllis McGinley, Peter Arno, William Steig, and Charles Addams (creator of the Addams Family).

In later decades, the editors of the magazine discovered and cultivated the work of many important twentieth century writers, such as J.D. Salinger, John Updike, and John Cheever. To be published in *The New Yorker* became a hallmark of literary success.

◆ Literary Works

Essay and Story Collections (illustrated with cartoons)
- *The Owl in the Attic* (1931)
- *The Seal in the Bedroom and Other Predicaments* (1932)
- *My Life and Hard Times* (1933)
- *The Last Flower* (1939)
- *Fables for Our Time* (1940)
- *My World—and Welcome to It* (1942)
- *The Thurber Carnival* (1945)
- *The Thurber Album* (1952)
- *Thurber's Dogs* (1955)
- *Alarms and Diversions* (1957)
- *The Years with Ross* (1959)
- *Lanterns and Lances* (1961)

Plays
- *Many Moons* (1947)
- *A Thurber Carnival* (1960)

Children's Books
- *Many Moons* (1943)
- *The Great Quillow* (1944)
- *The White Deer* (1945)
- *The 13 Clocks* (1950)
- *The Wonderful O* (1957)

*J*ames Thurber

from "Canines in the Cellar"

Number 921 South Champion Avenue is just another house now, in a long row of houses, but when we lived there, in 1899 and 1900, it was the last house on the street. Just south of us the avenue dwindled to a wood road that led into a thick grove of oak and walnut trees, long since destroyed by the southward march of asphalt. Our nearest neighbor on the north was fifty yards away, and across from us was a country meadow that ticked with crickets in the summertime and turned yellow with goldenrod in the fall. Living on the edge of town, we rarely heard footsteps at night, or carriage wheels, but the darkness, in every season, was deepened by the lonely sound of locomotive whistles. I no longer wonder, as I did when I was six, that Aunt Mary Van York, arriving at dusk for her first visit to us, looked about her disconsolately,[1] and said to my mother, "Why in the world do you want to live in this Godforsaken place, Mary?"

Almost all my memories of the Champion Avenue house have as their focal point the lively figure of my mother. I remember her tugging and hauling at a burning mattress and finally managing to shove it out a bedroom window onto the roof of the front porch, where it smoldered until my father came home from work and doused it with water. When he asked his wife how the mattress happened to catch fire, she told him the peculiar truth (all truths in that house were peculiar) that his youngest son, Robert, had set it on fire with a buggy whip. It seemed he had lighted the lash of the whip in the gas grate[2] of the nursery and applied it to the mattress. I also have a vivid memory of the night my mother was alone in the house with her three small sons and set the oil-splashed bowl of a kerosene lamp on fire, trying to light the wick, and herded all of us out of the house, announcing that it was going to explode. We children waited across the street in high anticipation, but the spilled oil burned itself out and, to our bitter disappointment, the house did not go up like a sky-rocket to scatter colored balloons among the stars. My mother claims that my brother William, who was seven at the time, kept crying, "Try it again, Mama, try it again," but she is a famous hand at ornamenting a tale,[3] and there is no way of telling whether he did or not.

---

1. disconsolately (dis kon′ sə lit lē): Sadly.
2. gas grate: In the early twentieth century, rooms were heated with gas fires behind metal grates.
3. a famous hand at ornamenting a tale: Well-known for adding to or exaggerating a story.

My brightest remembrance of the old house goes back to the confused and noisy second and last visit of Aunt Mary, who had cut her first visit short because she hated our two dogs—Judge, an irritable old pug, and Sampson, a restless water spaniel—and they hated her. She had snarled at them and they had growled at her all during her stay with us, and not even my mother remembers how she persuaded the old lady to come back for a weekend, but she did, and what is more, she cajoled[4] Aunt Mary into feeding "those dreadful brutes" the evening she arrived.

In preparation for this seemingly simple act of household routine, my mother had spent the afternoon gathering up all the dogs of the neighborhood, in advance of Aunt Mary's appearance, and putting them in the cellar. I had been allowed to go with her on her wonderful forays,[5] and I thought that we were going to keep all the sixteen dogs we rounded up. Such an adventure does not have to have logical point or purpose in the mind of a six-year-old, and I accepted as a remarkable but natural phenomenon my mother's sudden assumption of the stature of Santa Claus.

She did not always let my father in on her elaborate pranks, but he came home that evening to a house heavy with tension and suspense, and she whispered to him the peculiar truth that there were a dozen and a half dogs in the cellar, counting our Judge and Sampson. "What are you up to now, Mame?" he asked her, and she said she just wanted to see Aunt Mary's face when the dogs swarmed up into the kitchen. She could not recall where she had picked up all of the dogs, but I remembered, and still do, that we had imprisoned the Johnsons' Irish terrier, the Eiseles' shepherd, and the Mitchells' fox terrier, among others. "Well, let's get it over with, then," my father said nervously. "I want to eat dinner in peace, if that is possible."

The big moment finally arrived. My mother, full of smiles and insincerity, told Aunt Mary that it would relieve her of a tedious[6] chore—and heaven knows, she added, there were a thousand steps to take in that big house—if the old lady would be good enough to set down a plate of dog food in the kitchen at the head of the cellar stairs and call Judge and Sampson to their supper. Aunt Mary growled and grumbled, and consigned[7] all dogs to the fires of hell, but she grudgingly took the plate and carried it to the kitchen, with the Thurber family on her heels. "Heavenly days!" cried Aunt Mary. "Do you make a ceremony out of feeding these brutes?" She put the plate down and reached for the handle of the door.

---

4. cajoled (kə jōld′): Coaxed; persuaded by pleasant words, flattery, or false promises
5. forays (fōr′ āz): Raids.
6. tedious (tē′ dē əs): Tiresome.
7. consigned (kən sīnd′): Assigned; handed over.

None of us has ever been able to understand why bedlam[8] hadn't broken loose in the cellar long before this, but it hadn't. The dogs were probably so frightened by their unique predicament that their belligerence[9] had momentarily left them. But when the door opened and they could see the light of freedom and smell the odor of food, they gave tongue like a pack of hunting hounds. Aunt Mary got the door halfway open and the bodies of three of the largest dogs pushed it the rest of the way. There was a snarling, barking, yelping swirl of yellow and white, black and tan, gray and brindle as the dogs tumbled into the kitchen, skidded on the linoleum, sent the food flying from the plate, and backed Aunt Mary into a corner. "Great God Almighty!" she screamed. "It's a dog factory!" She was only five feet tall, but her counterattack was swift and terrible. Grabbing a broom, she opened the back door and the kitchen windows and began to beat and flail[10] at the army of canines, engaged now in half a dozen separate battles over the scattered food. Dogs flew out the back door and leaped through the windows, but some of them ran upstairs, and three or four others hid under sofas and chairs in the parlor. The indignant[11] snarling and cursing of Judge and Sampson rose above even the laughter of my mother and the delighted squeals of her children. Aunt Mary whammed her way from room to room, driving dogs ahead of her. When the last one had departed and the upset house had been put back in order, my father said to his wife, "Well, Mame, I hope you're satisfied." She was.

Aunt Mary, toward the end of her long life, got the curious notion that it was my father and his sons, and not my mother, who had been responsible for the noisy flux of "all those brutes." Years later, when we visited the old lady on one of her birthdays, she went over the story again, as she always did, touching it up with distortions and magnifications of her own. Then she looked at the male Thurbers in slow, rueful turn, sighed deeply, gazed sympathetically at my mother, and said, in her hollowest tone, "Poor Mary!"

---

8. bedlam (bed´ ləm): State of noisy confusion; uproar.
9. belligerence (bə lij´ ər əns): Aggressiveness; readiness to fight.
10. flail (flāl): To strike; beat; thresh.
11. indignant (in dig´ nənt): Angry at something unfair or mean.

☑ Check Your Comprehension

1. Describe the neighborhood around the Thurber house.
2. Why did Aunt Mary cut short her first visit to the Thurbers?
3. How do Thurber and his mother prepare for Aunt Mary's next visit?
4. What does Thurber's father say when his wife reveals the prank she has planned?
5. Describe what happens when Aunt Mary opens the cellar door.
6. Who does Aunt Mary later blame for the prank?

◆ Critical Thinking

INTERPRET

1. What do you think Thurber means when he says, at the beginning of the essay, that "all truths in that house were peculiar"? **[Interpret]**

2. What do the two family incidents described in the essay have in common? **[Connect]**

EVALUATE

3. What point of view do you think the author takes about these events from his childhood? Use details from the essay in your response. **[Evaluate]**

APPLY

4. How does Thurber portray his mother in this piece? Do you think Mary Thurber influenced her son to become a writer? If so, why? **[Speculate]**

EXTEND

5. Compare and contrast the impression of his family that Thurber presents in this essay with the impression of them he presents in "The Night the Bed Fell" on page 279 of *Prentice Hall Literature, Timeless Voices, Timeless Themes,* Bronze. **[Literary Link]**

James Thurber

Memorial

She came all the way from Illinois by train in a big wooden
crate many years ago, a frightened black poodle, not yet a year
old. She felt terrible in body and worse in mind. These contrap-
tions that men put on wheels, in contravention[1] of that law of
nature which holds that the feet must come in contact with the
ground in traveling, dismayed[2] her. She was never able to ride a
thousand yards in an automobile without getting sick at her
stomach, but she was always apologetic about this frailty, never,
as she might well have been, reproachful.[3]

She tried patiently at all times to understand Man's way of
life: the rolling of his wheels, the raising of his voice, the ringing
of his bells; his way of searching out with lights the dark protecting corners of the night; his habit of building his beds inside
walls, high above the nurturing earth. She refused, with all cour-
tesy, to accept his silly notion that it is better to bear puppies in
a place made of machined wood and clean blue cloth than in the
dark and warm dirt beneath the oak flooring of the barn.

The poodle was hand in glove[4] with natural phenomena. She
raised two litters of puppies, taking them in her stride, the way
she took the lightning and the snow. One of these litters, which
arrived ahead of schedule, was discovered under the barn floor
by a little girl of two. The child gaily displayed on her right fore-
arm the almost invisible and entirely painless marks of teeth
which had gently induced her to put down the live black toys she
had found and wanted to play with.

The poodle had no vices that I can think of, unless you could
count her incurable appetite for the tender tips of the young
asparagus in the garden and for the black raspberries when they
ripened on the bushes in the orchard. Sometimes, as punish-
ment for her depredations,[5] she walked into bees' nests or got
her long shaggy ears tangled in fence wire. She never snarled
about the penalties of existence or whimpered about the trials
and grotesqueries[6] of life with Man.

She accepted gracefully the indignities of the clipping machine
which, in her maiden days, periodically made a clown of her for
the dog shows, in accordance with the stupid and unimaginative

---

1. **contravention** (kon′ trə ven′ shən): Conflict; violation.
2. **dismayed** (dis mād′): Frightened; troubled.
3. **reproachful** (ri prōch′ fəl): Blaming; disapproving; resentful.
4. **hand in glove:** In harmony.
5. **depredations** (dep′ rə dā′ shənz): Robberies.
6. **grotesqueries** (grō tesk′ ər ēz): Unnatural or ridiculous actions.

notion that this most sensitive and dignified of animals is at heart a buffoon.[7] The poodle, which can look as husky as a Briard[8] when left shaggy, is an outdoor dog and can hold its own in the field with the best of the retrievers, including the Labrador.

The poodle won a great many ribbons in her bench days, but she would have traded all her medals for a dish of asparagus. She knew it was show time when the red rubber bib was tied around her neck. That meant a ride in a car to bedlam.[9]

Like the great Gammeyer of Tarkington's *Gentle Julia*, the poodle I knew seemed sometimes about to bridge the mysterious and conceivably narrow gap that separates instinct from reason. She could take part in your gaiety and your sorrow; she trembled to your uncertainties and lifted her head at your assurances. There were times when she seemed to come close to a pitying comprehension of the whole troubled scene and what lies behind it. If poodles, who walk so easily upon their hind legs, ever do learn the little tricks of speech and reason, I should not be surprised if they made a better job of it than Man, who would seem to be surely but not slowly slipping back to all fours.

The poodle kept her sight, her hearing, and her figure up to her quiet and dignified end. She knew that the Hand was upon her and she accepted it with a grave and unapprehensive resignation.[10] This, her dark intelligent eyes seemed to be trying to tell me, is simply the closing of full circle, this is the flower that grows out of Beginning; this—not to make it too hard for you, friend—is as natural as eating the raspberries and raising the puppies and riding into the rain.

---

7. **buffoon** (bə fōōn´): Clown; undignified person.
8. **Briard** (brē´ ärd): Breed of large, long-haired sheepdog, first bred in France.
9. **bedlam** (bed´ ləm): State of noisy confusion; uproar.
10. **resignation** (rez´ ig nā´ shən): Patient acceptance; quiet submission.

☑ **Check Your Comprehension**

1. What is the subject of this memorial tribute?
2. Which aspects of human life does the subject find hard to understand?
3. How does the subject behave at the end of her life?

◆ **Critical Thinking**

INTERPRET
1. What human qualities does the author attribute to the subject of his essay? **[Interpret]**

2. What does the author mean when he says that the subject "seemed sometimes about to bridge the mysterious and narrow gap that separates instinct from reason"? **[Interpret]**

EVALUATE
3. Why do you think the author says he wouldn't be surprised if poodles "made a better job of" speaking and reasoning than humans do? **[Analyze]**

APPLY
4. Have you ever had feelings similar to Thurber's about a pet or other animal? Explain. **[Relate]**

$\mathcal{J}$ ames Thurber

from The Pet Department

James Thurber was a keen observer of the newspapers and magazines of his day, and he often made fun of the clichéd writing he found there. Here, he creates a humorous advice column for pet owners.

Q. I enclose a sketch of the way my dog William has been lying for two days now. I think there must be something wrong with him. Can you tell me how to get him out of this?

MRS. L. L. G.

A. I should judge from the drawing that William is in a trance. Trance states, however, are rare with dogs. It may just be ecstasy. If at the end of another twenty-four hours he doesn't seem to be getting anywhere, I should give him up. The position of the ears leads me to believe that he may be enjoying himself in a quiet way, but the tail is somewhat alarming.

Q. No one has been able to tell us what kind of dog we have. I am enclosing a sketch of one of his two postures. He only has two. The other one is the same as this except he faces in the opposite direction.

MRS. EUGENIA BLACK

A. I think that what you have is a cast-iron lawn dog. The expressionless eye and the rigid pose are characteristic of metal lawn animals. And that certainly is a cast-iron ear. You could, however, remove all doubt by means of a simple test with a hammer and a cold chisel, or an acetylene torch. If the animal chips, or melts, my diagnosis is correct.

Q. Sometimes my dog does not seem to know me. I think he must be crazy. He will draw away, or show his fangs, when I approach him.

H. M. MORGAN, JR.

A. So would I, and I'm not crazy. If you creep up on your dog the way you indicate in the drawing, I can understand his viewpoint. Put your shirt in and straighten up; you look as if you had never seen a dog before, and that is undoubtedly what bothers the animal. These maladjustments can often be worked out by the use of a little common sense.

☑ Check Your Comprehension

1. What concern does Mrs. L. L. G. have about her pet, William? What is the expert's diagnosis of her problem?

2. What is Mrs. Eugenia Black trying to find out about her dog? What is the columnist's opinion, and what evidence does he or she offer?

3. Why does H. M. Morgan, Jr., write to The Pet Department? What advice does the columnist give?

◆ Critical Thinking

INTERPRET

1. Do you think that pet owners might write letters such as these to a pet expert? Why or why not? **[Infer]**

2. Which of the dogs diagnosed seems to have a problem that might really occur in real life? Why do you think so? **[Relate]**

3. How do the drawings enhance the writing in "The Pet Department"? Would the letters be as funny without them? Why? **[Analyze]**

EVALUATE

4. What is your opinion of the humor in "The Pet Department"? Explain why you do or do not find the letters funny. **[Evaluate]**

APPLY

5. Read the definition of irony on page 72. Choose one letter and reply from "The Pet Department," and identify how it is ironic. **[Apply]**

COMPARE LITERARY WORKS

6. In "Canines in the Cellar," Thurber's account of the trick Mrs. Thurber plays on Aunt Mary is humorous in a silly, slapstick way. In contrast, the humor in "The Pet Department" is ironic. How does Thurber's writing style achieve each effect? **[Analyze]**

$\mathcal{J}$ames Thurber
Comparing and Connecting the Author's Works

◆ Literary Focus: Irony

Thurber loved surprising his readers with unexpected twists on reality, contradictions that were sometimes funny, sometimes serious, and often both.

Irony is the name given to techniques that involve surprising, interesting, or amusing contradictions. In **irony of situation,** an event occurs that directly contradicts the expectations of the characters, the readers, or the audience.

For example, at the beginning of "Canines in the Cellar," Thurber describes the night his mother herded her sons out of the house after an accident with a kerosene lamp. Readers might expect that the young Thurber brothers would have been frightened. Instead, Thurber says, "We children waited across the street in high anticipation, but...to our bitter disappointment, the house did not go up like a skyrocket."

1. What ironic note, or surprising twist, does Thurber include at the end of "Canines in the Cellar"?
2. Most gardeners cross-breed flowers to improve them in some way. What is ironic about the crossbreeds Hyde produces in *The Wonderful O*?
3. According to "Memorial," what is ironic about the way that poodles are clipped and presented in dog shows?

◆ Drawing Conclusions About Thurber's Work

The selections you have read depict two different kinds of heroic figures:

1. a lively, dramatic mother in "Canines in the Cellar"
2. a gentle, dignified dog in "Memorial"

What qualities does Thurber find inspiring and admirable in these three fig-

ures? Below is a cluster diagram that explores some of the qualities Mrs. Thurber demonstrates in "Canines in the Cellar." Create a similar cluster diagram for the poodle in "Memorial." Then share and compare your work in a class discussion. Do the figures share any qualities, or do they represent completely different kinds of heroes for Thurber?

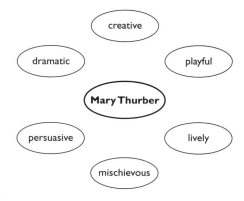

◆ Idea Bank

Writing

1. **Memorial Tribute** Write your own tribute to a pet, pointing out the animal's best qualities. Your tribute may be serious, funny, or a combination of both. Read the tribute aloud to your classmates.
2. **Advice Column** Write your own humorous advice column in a topic area of your choice. Before you begin, review advice columns in newspapers and magazines, and decide which of their features might be exaggerated with comic effects.

Speaking and Listening

3. **Oral Interpretation** In a group, present the central events in "Canines in the Cellar" as a play. Reread the selection, and prepare a script. Add

further dialogue if you wish. After rehearsing, perform the piece for the class as a whole. **[Performing Arts Link]**

Researching and Representing

4. **Chart on Animal Intelligence** In "Memorial" Thurber attributes great intelligence and deep emotions to his dog. Using magazines or the Internet, research the latest scientific findings about the intelligence and emotions of various animals, both wild and domestic. Prepare a chart to display your findings. **[Science Link]**

5. **Illustrations** Find books containing Thurber's drawings of dogs. Then draw your own illustrations for "Memorial" or "Canines in the Cellar," either in Thurber's style or in your own. **[Art Link]**

◆ Further Reading, Listening, and Viewing

- Thurber, James. *My Life and Hard Times* (1933). This hilarious volume of autobiographical essays describing Thurber's eccentric Columbus family includes the classics "The Night the Bed Fell" and "The Night the Ghost Got In."

- Thurber, James. *Thurber's Dogs* (1955). Enjoy more of Thurber's essays and drawings devoted to dogs in this volume, which includes "Memorial" and "Canines in the Cellar."

- Thurber, James. *The Wonderful O* (1957). Evil pirates have banned the use of the letter *o* on the island of Ooroo. An intriguing tale of humble villagers living lives minus o-words.

- *The 13 Clock* (1994). This audiocassette presents Thurber's magical fairy tale about the courtship of Prince Norna and Princess Saralina, read by actor Edward Woodward.

- *The Secret Life of Walter Mitty* (1947). This movie version of Thurber's famous story stars Danny Kaye as the meek little man who escapes into daydreams of heroic fantasy.

On the Web:

http://www.phschool.com/atschool/literature
Go to the student edition *Bronze*. Proceed to Unit 4. Then click Hot Links to find Web sites featuring James Thurber.

James Herriot In Depth

> "I've lived in this beautiful district, having the great pleasure of being associated with animals. Oh aye, it's been a marvelous life."
>
> —*James Herriot*

JAMES HERRIOT drew on his experiences as a country veterinarian to create warm and lively stories that became worldwide bestsellers. His love of animals shines through in his simple, moving tales. His works gained even greater renown when they became the basis for a television series. Even at the height of his fame, Herriot never abandoned his animal patients.

A Childhood Dream Comes True

Herriot spent a happy childhood in Hillhead, Scotland, a small town near Glasgow. He was born James Alfred Wight, and used the name Herriot only to publish his books. He fondly remembers spending long walks with his dog, "camping and climbing among the highlands of Scotland so that at an early age three things were implanted in my character: a love of animals, reading, and the countryside."

At the age of thirteen, Herriot decided he wanted to be a veterinarian. With determination and strong dedication, he graduated from Glasgow Veterinary School.

A Different Kind of Vet

At school, Herriot always imagined he would have his own modern practice. He thought he would handle mostly pet cats and dogs. However, in the middle of the Great Depression, jobs were scarce. Herriot finally found a position as an assistant vet in North Yorkshire, a remote and rural area of England.

Instead of cats and dogs, Herriot found himself treating mostly farm animals: horses, pigs, cows, sheep, and other livestock. His early experiences opened his eyes to a new world of animals and veterinary medicine. He soon fell in love with his job and Yorkshire itself, learning that "treating cows and pigs and sheep and horses had a fascination I had never even suspected; and this brought with it a new concept of myself as a tiny wheel in the great machine of British agriculture."

Family Life Interrupted by War

In 1941, Herriot married and became a full partner in the Yorkshire veterinary practice with his former employer, Siegfried Farnon. In his best-selling book *All Creatures Great and Small,* Herriot describes the joys of his early years as a vet. He describes everything from helping cows give birth to treating Tricki Woo, a pampered Pekinese dog.

In 1943, Herriot was called up to serve in the war. For the rest of World War II, he served in the Royal Air Force. Though he was stationed in Scarborough, not too far from his home, he was overjoyed to return to his wife and patients as soon as the war ended.

Responding to a Dare

Throughout his life, Herriot was well-known for his engaging stories. He often came home from work and told his wife amusing tales of the animals and people of the day. Laughing, he would often add that he was saving the stories for the book that he would write some day. One day, Mrs. Herriot replied, "Who are you kidding? Vets of fifty don't write first books." Stung, Herriot rose to the challenge. He promptly bought some paper and began to learn how to type.

A New Career and a New Name

Herriot's first attempts to write down his stories were amateurish and flat, but he did not give up. He worked hard to learn the craft of writing. Soon, the quality of his writing improved. He learned to capture the surprises and pleasures of his veterinary work in clear, straightforward prose.

At that time, British veterinarians were not allowed to advertise. Worried that stories based on his own experiences might seem like advertising, James Alfred Wight decided to use the name James Herriot as a writer's pseudonym, or pen name.

Audience and Patients People all over the world love Herriot's tales. His books have sold over fifty million copies worldwide.

Herriot continued his veterinary practice into his seventies, treating his animal patients and signing autographs for his many fans. He turned some of his most memorable tales into children's books to share them with an even wider audience.

Lasting Legacies Herriot's life and works live on in many ways. In addition to his many books, fans enjoy watching the television series based on his books, *All Creatures Great and Small*.

Herriot's son, Jim Wight, continued in his father's footsteps, becoming a vet and joining the Yorkshire practice.

◆ Veterinary Medicine

Like doctors who treat humans, veterinarians go through a challenging and strict education. Most vets specialize in small animals, such as house pets, or in treating large animals, such as horses and other farm animals. Herriot's practice was particularly unusual because he treated animals "great and small," from parakeets to horses.

Many of Herriot's tales describe the early days of his practice during the 1940's and 1950's. Veterinary medicine was not nearly as sophisticated in those days as it is today. Herriot had very little modern equipment to work with. Instead, he had to combine his knowledge of animals with common sense. His natural optimism certainly helped him make the best of a difficult situation. "We had no antibiotics, few drugs," he remembers "A lot of time was spent pouring things down cows' throats."

Although the technology has changed, people are still drawn to the career of veterinarian for the same reasons as James Herriot was. As a child, he had read a magazine article about a veterinarian at work and was inspired to seek a career treating sick animals. Today, many vets receive a first glimpse of their future careers when they start to read Herriot's inspiring stories. In fact, one veterinarian has paid tribute to Herriot's influence on her choice of career by creating a web site honoring his life and works.

◆ Literary Works

Novels
- *All Creatures Great and Small* (1972)
- *All Things Bright and Beautiful* (1974)
- *All Things Wise and Wonderful* (1977)

Collections
- *James Herriot's Dog Stories* (1986)
- *James Herriot's Cat Stories* (1994)

Nonfiction
- *James Herriot's Yorkshire* (1979)

For Children
- *Moses the Kitten* (1984)
- *Only One Woof* (1985)
- *The Christmas Day Kitten* (1986)
- *The Market Square Dog* (1990)

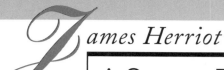

A Spot or Two of Bother

I am never at my best in the early morning, especially the cold mornings you get in Yorkshire when a piercing wind sweeps down from the fells, finding its way inside clothing, nipping at noses and ears. It was a cheerless time, and a particularly bad time to be standing in this cobbled farmyard watching a beautiful horse dying because of my incompetence.[1]

It had started at eight o'clock. Mr. Kettlewell telephoned as I was finishing my breakfast.

"I 'ave a fine big cart 'oss here and he's come out in spots."

"Really? What kind of spots?"

"Well, round and flat, and they're all over 'im."

"And it started quite suddenly?"

"Aye, he were right as rain last night."

"All right, I'll have a look at him right away." I nearly rubbed my hands. Urticaria. It usually cleared up spontaneously, but an injection hastened the process and I had a new antihistamine drug to try out—it was said to be specific for this sort of thing. Anyway, it was the kind of situation where it was easy for the vet to look good. A nice start to the day.

In the fifties, the tractor had taken over most of the work on the farms, but there was still a fair number of draft horses around, and when I arrived at Mr. Kettlewell's place I realized that this one was something special.

The farmer was leading him from a loose box into the yard. A magnificent Shire, all of eighteen hands, with a noble head which he tossed proudly as he paced toward me. I appraised him with something like awe, taking in the swelling curve of the neck, the deep-chested body, the powerful limbs abundantly feathered above the massive feet.

"What a wonderful horse!" I gasped. "He's enormous!"

Mr Kettlewell smiled with quiet pride. "Aye, he's a right smasher. I only bought 'im last month. I do like to have a good 'oss about."

He was a tiny man, elderly but sprightly, and one of my favorite farmers. He had to reach high to pat the huge neck and was nuzzled in return. "He's kind, too. Right quiet."

"Ah well, it's worth a lot when a horse is good-natured as well as good-looking." I ran my hand over the typical plaques in the skin. "Yes, this is urticaria, all right."

"What's that?"

---

1. **incompetence:** Lack of ability.

"Sometimes it's called nettle rash. It's an allergic condition. He may have eaten something unusual, but it's often difficult to pinpoint the cause."

"Is it serious?"

"Oh no. I have an injection that'll soon put him right. He's well enough in himself, isn't he?"

"Aye, right as a bobbin."

"Good. Sometimes it upsets an animal, but this fellow's the picture of health."

As I filled my syringe with the antihistamine I felt that I had never spoken truer words. The big horse radiated health and well-being.

He did not move as I gave the injection, and I was about to put my syringe away when I had another thought. I had always used a proprietary[2] preparation for urticaria and it had invariably worked. Maybe it would be a good idea to supplement the antihistamine, just to make sure. I wanted a good, quick cure for this splendid horse.

I trotted back to my car to fetch the old standby and injected the usual dose. Again the big animal paid no attention and the farmer laughed.

"By gaw, he doesn't mind, does 'e?"

I pocketed the syringe. "No, I wish all our patients were like him. He's a grand sort."

This, I thought, was vetting at its best. An easy trouble-free case, a nice farmer and a docile[3] patient who was a picture of equine[4] beauty, a picture I could have looked at all day. I didn't want to go away although other calls were waiting. I just stood there, half listening to Mr. Kettlewell's chatter about the imminent[5] lambing season.

"Ah well," I said at length, "I must be on my way." I was turning to go when I noticed that the farmer had fallen silent.

The silence lasted for a few moments, then, "He's dotherin' a bit," he said.

I looked at the horse. There was the faintest tremor in the muscles of the limbs. It was hardly visible, but as I watched, it began to spread upward, bit by bit, until the skin over the neck, body and rump began to quiver. It was very slight, but there was no doubt it was gradually increasing in intensity.

"What is it?" said Mr. Kettlewell.

"Oh, just a little reaction. It'll soon pass off." I was trying to sound airy, but I wasn't so sure.

---

2. **proprietary** (prō prī´ ə tār ē): Produced by one manufacturer; a proprietary drug has no direct competition, because it is only produced by one company.
3. **docile** (das´ əl): Mild-mannered, peaceful.
4. **equine** (ē´ kwīn): Of or relating to horses.
5. **imminent:** Upcoming; near.

With agonizing slowness the trembling developed into a generalized shaking of the entire frame and this steadily increased in violence as the farmer and I stood there in silence. I seemed to have been there a long time, trying to look calm and unworried, but I couldn't believe what I was seeing. This sudden inexplicable[6] transition—there was no reason for it. My heart began to thump and my mouth turned dry as the shaking was replaced by great shuddering spasms which racked[7] the horse's frame, and his eyes, so serene a short while ago, started from his head in terror, while foam began to drop from his lips. My mind raced. Maybe I shouldn't have mixed those injections, but it couldn't have this fearful effect. It was impossible.

As the seconds passed, I felt I couldn't stand much more of this. The blood hammered in my ears. Surely he would start to recover soon—he couldn't get worse.

I was wrong. Almost imperceptibly[8] the huge animal began to sway. Only a little at first, then more and more until he was tilting from side to side like a mighty oak in a gale. Oh, dear God, he was going to go down and that would be the end. And that end had to come soon. Even the cobbles seemed to shake under my feet as the great horse crashed to the ground. For a few moments he lay there, stretched on his side, his feet pedaling convulsively, then he was still.

Well, that was it. I had killed this magnificent horse. It was impossible, unbelievable that a few minutes ago that animal had been standing there in all his strength and beauty and I had come along with my clever new medicines and now there he was, dead.

What was I going to say? I'm terribly sorry, Mr. Kettlewell, I just can't understand how this happened. My mouth opened, but nothing came out, not even a croak. And, as though looking at a picture from the outside I became aware of the square of farm buildings with the dark, snow-streaked fells rising behind under a lowering sky, of the biting wind, the farmer and myself, and the motionless body of the horse.

I felt chilled to the bone and miserable, but I had to say my piece. I took a long, quavering breath and was about to speak when the horse raised his head slightly. I said nothing, nor did Mr. Kettlewell, as the big animal eased himself onto his chest, looked around him for a few seconds, then got to his feet. He shook his head, then walked across to his master. The recovery was just as quick, just as incredible, as the devastating collapse, and he showed no ill effects from his crashing fall onto the cobbled yard.

---

6. **inexplicable** (in eks′ pli kə bəl): Unexplainable.
7. **racked:** Convulsed.
8. **imperceptibly** (im pər sep′ tə blī): Undetectably; unnoticeably.

The farmer reached up and patted the horse's neck. "You know, Mr. Herriot, them spots have nearly gone!"

I went over and had a look. "That's right. You can hardly see them now."

Mr. Kettlewell shook his head wonderingly. "Aye, well, it's a wonderful new treatment. But I'll tell tha summat. I hope you don't mind me sayin' this, but," he put his hand on my arm and looked up into my face, "ah think it's just a bit drastic."

I drove away from the farm and pulled up the car in the lee of a drystone wall. A great weariness had descended upon me. This sort of thing wasn't good for me. I was getting on in years now—well into my thirties—and I couldn't stand these shocks like I used to. I tipped the driving mirror down and had a look at myself. I was a bit pale, but not as ghastly white as I felt. Still, the feeling of guilt and bewilderment persisted, and with it the recurring[9] thought that there must be easier ways of earning a living than as a country veterinary surgeon. Twenty-four hours a day, seven days a week, rough, dirty and peppered with traumatic incidents like that near catastrophe back there. I leaned back against the seat and closed my eyes.

When I opened them a few minutes later, the sun had broken through the clouds, bringing the green hillsides and the sparkling ridges of snow to vivid life, painting the rocky outcrops with gold. I wound down the window and breathed in the cold clean air drifting down, fresh and tangy, from the moorland high above.

Peace began to steal through me. Maybe I hadn't done anything wrong with Mr. Kettlewell's horse. Maybe antihistamines did sometimes cause these reactions. Anyway, as I started the engine and drove away, the old feeling began to well up in me and within moments it was running strong: it was good to be able to work with animals in this thrilling countryside; I was lucky to be a vet in the Yorkshire Dales.

---

9. **recurring:** Returning; frequent.

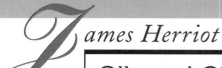

Olly and Ginny:
Two Kittens Who Came to Stay

"Look at that, Jim! Surely that's a stray cat. I've never seen it before." Helen was at the kitchen sink, washing dishes, and she pointed through the window.

Our new house in Hannerly had been built into a sloping field. There was a low retaining[1] wall, chest high, just outside the window and, behind, the grassy bank led from the wall top up to some bushes and an open log shed perched about twenty yards away. A lean little cat was peering warily from the bushes. Two tiny kittens crouched by her side.

"I think you're right," I said. "That's a stray with her family and she's looking for food."

Helen put out a bowl of meat scraps and some milk on the flat top of the wall and retired to the kitchen. The mother cat did not move for a few minutes, then she advanced with the utmost[2] caution, took up some of the food in her mouth and carried it back to her kittens.

Several times she crept down the bank, but when the kittens tried to follow her, she gave them a quick "get back" tap with her paw.

We watched, fascinated, as the scraggy, half-starved creature made sure that her family had eaten before she herself took anything from the bowl. Then, when the food was finished, we quietly opened the back door. But as soon as they saw us, cat and kittens flitted away into the field.

"I wonder where they came from," Helen said.

I shrugged. "Heaven knows. There's a lot of open country round here. They could have come from miles away. And that mother cat doesn't look like an ordinary stray. There's a real wild look about her."

Helen nodded. "Yes, she looks as though she's never been in a house, never had anything to do with people. I've heard of wild cats like that who live outside. Maybe she only came looking for food because of her kittens."

"I think you're right," I said as we returned to the kitchen. "Anyway, the poor little things have had a good feed. I don't suppose we'll see them again."

But I was wrong. Two days later, the trio reappeared. In the same place, peeping from the bushes, looking hungrily towards the kitchen window. Helen fed them again, the mother cat still

---

1. **retaining:** Holding.
2. **utmost:** Greatest.

fiercely forbidding her kittens to leave the bushes, and once more they darted away when we tried to approach them. When they came again next morning, Helen turned to me and smiled.

"I think we've been adopted," she said.

She was right. The three of them took up residence in the log shed and after a few days the mother allowed the kittens to come down to the food bowls, shepherding them carefully all the way. They were still quite tiny, only a few weeks old. One was black and white, the other tortoiseshell.

Helen fed them for a fortnight,[3] but they remained unapproachable creatures. Then one morning, as I was about to go on my rounds, she called me into the kitchen.

She pointed through the window. "What do you make of that?"

I looked and saw the two kittens in their usual position under the bushes, but there was no mother cat.

"That's strange," I said. "She's never let them out of her sight before."

The kittens had their feed and I tried to follow them as they ran away, but I lost them in the long grass, and although I searched all over the field there was no sign of them or their mother.

We never saw the mother cat again and Helen was quite upset.

"What on earth can have happened to her?" she murmured a few days later as the kittens ate their morning meal.

"Could be anything," I replied. "I'm afraid the mortality rate for wandering cats is very high. She could have been run over by a car or had some other accident. I'm afraid we'll never know."

Helen looked again at the little creatures crouched side by side, their heads in the bowl. "Do you think she's just abandoned them?"

"Well, it's possible. She was a maternal and caring little thing and I have a feeling she looked around till she could find a good home for them. She didn't leave till she saw that they could fend for themselves and maybe she's returned to her outside life now. She was a real wild one."

It remained a mystery, but one thing was sure: the kittens were installed for good. Another thing was sure: they would never be domesticated. Try as we might, we were never able to touch them, and all our attempts to wheedle[4] them into the house were unavailing.[5]

One wet morning, Helen and I looked out of the kitchen window at the two of them sitting on the wall, waiting for their breakfast, their fur sodden, their eyes nearly closed against the driving rain.

---

3. **fortnight:** Two weeks.
4. **wheedle:** Coax; charm someone into doing something.
5. **unavailing:** Futile; unproductive.

"Poor little things," Helen said, "I can't bear to see them out there, wet and cold, we *must* get them inside."

"How? We've tried often enough."

"Oh, I know, but let's have another go. Maybe they'll be glad to come in out of the rain."

We mashed up a dish of fresh fish, an irresistible delicacy to cats. I let them have a sniff and they were eager and hungry, then I placed the dish just inside the back door before retreating out of sight. But as we watched through the window the two of them sat motionless in the downpour, their eyes fixed on the fish, but determined not to go through the door. That, clearly, was unthinkable.

"All right, you win," I said and put the food on the wall where it was immediately devoured.

I was staring at them with a feeling of defeat when Herbert Platt, one of the local dustmen, came round the corner. At the sight of him the kittens scurried away and Herbert laughed.

"Ah see you've taken on them cats. That's some nice stuff they're gettin' to eat."

"Yes, but they won't come inside to get it."

He laughed again. "Aye, and they never will, Ah've know'n that family o' cats for years, and all their ancestors. I saw that mother cat when she first came, and before that she lived at awd Mrs. Caley's over the hill and ah remember that 'un's mother before her, down at Billy Tate's farm. Ah can go back donkey's years with them cats."

"Gosh, is that so?"

"Aye, it is, and I've never seen one o' that strain that would go inside a house. They're wild, real wild."

"Ah well, thanks Herbert, that explains a lot."

He smiled and hoisted a bin. "Ah'll get off, then, and they can finish their breakfast."

"Well, that's it, Helen," I said. "Now we know. They're always going to be outside, but at least we can try to improve their accommodation."

The thing we called the log shed, where I had laid some straw for them to sleep, wasn't a shed at all. It had a roof, but was open all down one side, with widely spaced slats on the other three sides. It allowed a constant through-wind which made it a fine place for drying out the logs but horribly draughty[6] as a dwelling.

I went up the grassy slope and put up a sheet of plywood as a wind-break. Then I built up a mound of logs into a protective zariba[7] around the straw bed and stood back, puffing slightly.

"Right," I said. "They'll be quite cozy in there now."

---

6. **draughty** (draf´ tē): Drafty.
7. **zariba** (zə rī´ bə): A protective wall, usually made of thorny bushes.

Helen nodded in agreement, but she had gone one better. Behind my wind-break, she put down an open-sided box with cushions inside. "There now, they needn't sleep on the straw any more. They'll be warm and comfortable in this nice box."

I rubbed my hands. "Great. We won't have to worry about them in bad weather. They'll really enjoy coming in here."

From that moment the kittens boycotted the shed. They still came for their meals every day, but we never saw them anywhere near their old dwelling.

"They're just not used to it," Helen said.

"Hmm." I looked again at the cushioned box tucked in the centre of the encircling logs. "Either that, or they don't like it."

We stuck it out for a few days, then, as we wondered where on earth the kittens could be sleeping, our resolve began to crack. I went up the slope and dismantled the wall of logs. Immediately the two little creatures returned. They sniffed and nosed round the box and went away again.

"I'm afraid they're not keen on your box either," I grunted as we watched from our vantage point.

Helen looked stricken. "Silly little things. It's perfect for them."

But after another two days during which the shed lay deserted, she went out and I saw her coming sadly down the bank, box in one hand, cushions under her arm.

The kittens were back within hours, looking round the place, vastly relieved. They didn't seem to object to the wind-break and settled happily in the straw. Our attempts to produce a feline Hilton had been a total failure.

It dawned on me that they couldn't bear to be enclosed, to have their escape routes cut off. Lying there on the open bed of straw, they could see all around them and were able to flit away between the slats at the slightest sign of danger.

"Okay, my friends," I said, "that's the way you want it, but I'm going to find out something more about you."

Helen gave them some food and once they were concentrating on the food, I crept up on them and threw a fisherman's landing net over them and after a struggle I was able to divine that the tortoiseshell was a female and the black and white a male.

"Good," said Helen, "I'll call them Olly and Ginny."

"Why Olly?"

"Don't really know. He looks like an Olly. I like the name."

"Oh, and how about Ginny?"

"Short for Ginger."

"She's not really ginger, she's tortoiseshell."

"Well, she's a bit ginger."

I left it at that.

Over the next few months they grew rapidly and my veterinary mind soon reached a firm decision. I had to neuter them. And it was then that I was confronted for the first time with a problem which was to worry me for years—how to minister to the veterinary needs of animals which I was unable even to touch.

The first time, when they were half grown, it wasn't so bad. Again I slunk up on them with my net when they were feeding and managed to bundle them into a cat cage from which they looked at me with terrified and, I imagined, accusing eyes.

In the surgery, as Siegfried and I lifted them one by one from the cage and administered the intravenous anesthetic, I was struck by the fact that although they were terror-stricken at being in an enclosed space for the first time in their lives and by being grasped and restrained by humans, they were singularly easy to handle. Many of our domesticated feline patients were fighting furies until we had lulled them to sleep, and cats, with claws as well as teeth for weapons, can inflict a fair amount of damage. However, Olly and Ginny, although they struggled frantically, made no attempt to bite, never unsheathed their claws.

Siegfried put it briefly. "These little things are scared stiff, but they're absolutely docile. I wonder how many wild cats are like this."

I felt a little strange as I carried out the operations, looking down at the small sleeping forms. These were my cats yet it was the first time I was able to touch them as I wished, examine them closely, appreciate the beauty of their fur and colourings.

When they had come out of the anaesthetic, I took them home and when I released the two of them from the cage, they scampered up to their home in the log shed. As was usual following such minor operations, they showed no after effects, but they clearly had unpleasant memories of me. During the next few weeks they came close to Helen as she fed them but fled immediately at the sight of me. All my attempts to catch Ginny to remove the single little stitch in her spay incision were fruitless. That stitch remained for ever and I realised that Herriot had been cast firmly as the villain of the piece, the character who would grab you and bundle you into a wire cage if you gave him half a chance.

It soon became clear that things were going to stay that way because, as the months passed and Helen plied them with all manner of titbits and they grew into truly handsome, sleek cats, they would come arching along the wall top when she appeared at the back door, but I had only to poke my head from the door to send them streaking away out of sight. I was the chap to be avoided at all times, and this rankled with me because I have always been fond of cats and I had become particularly attached to these two. The day finally arrived when Helen was able to stroke them gently as they ate and my chagrin[8] deepened at the sight.

---

8. **chagrin:** Embarrassment.

Usually they slept in the log shed but occasionally they disappeared to somewhere unknown and stayed away for a few days, and we used to wonder if they had abandoned us or if something had happened to them. When they reappeared, Helen would shout to me in great relief, "They're back, Jim, they're back!" They had become part of our lives.

Summer lengthened into autumn and when the bittter Yorkshire winter set in we marvelled at their hardiness. We used to feel terrible, looking at them from our warm kitchen as they sat out in the frost and snow, but no matter how harsh the weather, nothing would induce either of them to set foot inside the house. Warmth and comfort had no appeal to them.

When the weather was fine we had a lot of fun just watching them. We could see right up into the log shed from our kitchen, and it was fascinating to observe their happy relationship. They were such friends. Totally inseparable, they spent hours licking each other and rolling about together in gentle play and they never pushed each other out of the way when they were given their food. At nights we could see the two furry little forms curled close together in the straw.

Then there was a time when we thought everything had changed forever. The cats did one of their disappearing acts and as day followed day we became more anxious. Each morning, Helen started her day with the cry of "Olly, Ginny" which always brought the two of them trotting down from their dwelling, but now they did not appear, and when a week passed and then two we had almost run out of hope.

When we came back from our half day in Brawton,[9] Helen ran to the kitchen and looked out. The cats knew our habits and they would always be sitting waiting for her but the empty wall stretched away and the log shed was deserted. "Do you think they've gone for good, Jim?" she said.

I shrugged. "It's beginning to look like it. You remember what old Herbert said about that family of cats. Maybe they're nomads at heart—gone off to pastures new."

Helen's face was doleful.[10] "I can't believe it. They seemed so happy here. Oh, I hope nothing terrible has happened to them." Sadly she began to put her shopping away and she was silent all evening. My attempts to cheer her up were half-hearted because I was wrapped in a blanket of misery myself.

Strangely, it was the very next morning when I heard Helen's usual cry, but this time it wasn't a happy one.

---

9. **half day in Brawton:** Afternoon off in a nearby town.
10. **doleful:** Sad; mournful.

She ran into the sitting room. "They're back, Jim," she said breathlessly, "but I think they're dying!"

"What? What do you mean?"

"Oh, they look awful! They're desperately ill—I'm sure they're dying."

I hurried through to the kitchen with her and looked through the window. The cats were sitting there side by side on the wall a few feet away. A watery discharge ran from their eyes, which were almost closed, more fluid poured from their nostrils and saliva drooled from their mouths. Their bodies shook from a continuous sneezing and coughing.

They were thin and scraggy, unrecognisable as the sleek creatures we knew so well, and their appearance was made more pitiful by their situation in the teeth of a piercing east wind which tore at their fur and made their attempts to open their eyes even more painful.

Helen opened the back door. "Olly, Ginny, what's happened to you?" she cried softly.

A remarkable thing then happened. At the sound of her voice, the cats hopped carefully from the wall and walked unhesitatingly through the door into the kitchen. It was the first time they had been under our roof.

"Look at that!" Helen exclaimed. "I can't believe it. They must be really ill. But what is it, Jim? Have they been poisoned?"

I shook my head. "No, they've got cat flu."

"You can tell?"

"Oh, yes, this is classical."

"And will they die?"

I rubbed my chin. "I don't think so." I wanted to sound reassuring, but I wondered. Feline virus rhinotracheitis had a fairly low mortality rate, but bad cases can die and these cats were very bad indeed. "Anyway, close the door, Helen, and I'll see if they'll let me examine them."

But at the sight of the closing door, both cats bolted back outside.

"Open up again," I cried and, after a moment's hesitation, the cats walked back into the kitchen.

I looked at them in astonishment. "Would you believe it? They haven't come in here for shelter, they've come for help!"

And there was no doubt about it. The two of them sat there, side by side, waiting for us to do something for them.

"The question is," I said, "will they allow their bête noire[11] to get near them? We'd better leave the back door open so they don't feel threatened."

---

11. **bête noire** (bet nwär´): Someone or something that is particularly hated or detested.

I approached inch by inch until I could put a hand on them, but they did not move. With a feeling that I was dreaming, I lifted each of them, limp and unresisting, and examined them.

Helen stroked them while I ran out to my car which held my stock of drugs and brought in what I'd need. I took their temperatures, they were both over 104, which was typical. Then I injected them with oxytetracycline, the antibiotic which I had always found best for treating the secondary bacterial infection which followed the initial virus attack. I also injected vitamins, cleaned away the pus and mucus from the eyes and nostrils with cotton wool and applied an antibiotic ointment. And all the time I marvelled that I was lifting and handling these yielding little bodies which I hadn't even been able to touch before apart from when they had been under the anaesthetic for the neutering ops.

When I had finished I couldn't bear the thought of turning them out into that cruel wind. I lifted them up and tucked them one under each arm.

"Helen," I said, "let's have another try. Will you just gently close the door."

She took hold of the knob and began to push very slowly, but immediately both cats leaped like uncoiled springs from my arms and shot into the garden. We watched them as they trotted out of sight.

"Well, that's extraordinary," I said. "Ill as they are, they won't tolerate being shut in."

Helen was on the verge of tears. "But how will they stand it out there? They should be kept warm. I wonder if they'll stay now or will they leave us again."

"I just don't know." I looked at the empty garden. "But we've got to realise they are in their natural environment. They're tough little things. I think they'll be back."

I was right. Next morning they were outside the window, eyes closed against the wind, the fur on their faces streaked and stained with the copious[12] discharge.

Again Helen opened the door and again they walked calmly inside and made no resistance as I repeated my treatment, injecting them, swabbing out eyes and nostrils, examining their mouths for ulcers, lifting them around like any long-standing household pets.

This happened every day for a week. The discharges became more purulent[13] and their racking sneezing seemed no better; then, when I was losing hope, they started to eat a little food and, significantly, they weren't so keen to come into the house.

When I did get them inside, they were tense and unhappy as I handled them and finally I couldn't touch them at all. They were

12. **copious:** Abundant; plentiful.
13. **purulent:** Badly infected.

by no means cured, so I mixed oxytet soluble powder in their food and treated them that way.

The weather was even worse, with fine flakes of snow spinning in the wind, but the day came when they refused to come inside and we watched them through the window as they ate. But I had the satisfaction of knowing they were still getting the antibiotic with every mouthful.

As I carried on this long-range treatment, observing them daily from the kitchen, it was rewarding to see the sneezing abating, the discharges drying up and the cats gradually regaining their lost flesh.

It was a brisk sunny morning in March and I was watching Helen putting their breakfast on the wall. Olly and Ginny, sleek as seals, their faces clean and dry, their eyes bright, came arching along the wall, purring like outboard motors. They were in no hurry to eat; they were clearly happy just to see her.

As they passed to and fro, she ran her hand gently along their heads and backs. This was the kind of stroking they liked—not overdone, with them continually in motion.

I felt I had to get into the action and stepped from the open door.

"Ginny," I said and held out a hand. "Come here, Ginny." The little creature stopped her promenade along the wall and regarded me from a safe distance, not with hostility but with all the old wariness. As I tried to move nearer to her, she skipped away out of reach.

"Okay," I said, "and I don't suppose it's any good trying with you either, Olly." The black-and-white cat backed well away from my outstretched hand and gave me a non-committal gaze. I could see he agreed with me.

Mortified, I called out to the two of them. "Hey, remember me?" It was clear by the look of them that they remembered me all right—but not in the way I hoped. I felt a stab of frustration. Despite my efforts I was back where I started.

Helen laughed. "They're a funny pair, but don't they look marvellous! They're a picture of health, as good as new. It says a lot for fresh air treatment."

"It does indeed," I said with a wry smile, "but it also says something for having a resident veterinary surgeon."

☑ **Check Your Comprehension**

1. Why does Mr. Kettlewell call Herriot?
2. What effect does Herriot's treatment have on Mr. Kettlewell's horse?
3. Describe two ways in which Olly and Ginny are unlike typical pet cats.
4. How does the cats' behavior change when they become ill?

◆ **Critical Thinking**

INTERPRET

1. As a vet, Herriot must constantly adjust his treatment strategies to suit each patient. What unusual steps does he take to treat Olly and Ginny? **[Classify]**
2. Why is Herriot surprised by the results of the medicine he gives to Kettlewell's horse? **[Infer]**

3. Describe Herriot's attitude toward his work and tell how it helps him to treat animals successfully. **[Draw Conclusions]**

COMPARE LITERARY WORKS

4. Do you think Herriot learns more about being an effective vet by treating Olly and Ginny or by injecting Mr. Kettlewell's horse? Explain your answer. **[Compare and Contrast]**

APPLY

5. Name three subjects Herriot would have had to study to become a successful veterinarian. Use details from the story to support your answer. **[Career Link]**

$\mathcal{J}$ ames Herriot
Comparing and Connecting the Author's Works

◆ Literary Focus: Observation

James Herriot was a keen observer of animals and of human beings, and many of his writings function as observations. In an **observation,** a writer describes an event he or she saw firsthand and might have watched over an extended period of time. The writer includes many details and chooses vivid, precise words to recreate the event for the reader. Observations often focus on scientific phenomena, such as the behavior of a wild animal or the outcome of an experiment. As a veterinarian, most of James Herriot's observations are of animals and of the progression of their illnesses and treatments. He describes the process of his treatment of an animal in such vivid detail that readers feel as though they are looking over his shoulder as he works.

Main Features of an Observation

• Describes an event the author witnessed firsthand

• Includes many details

• Uses vivid, precise words

1. Reread "A Spot or Two of Bother," and compare the passages that describe Herriot's and Kettlewell's responses to events. Are these passages similar to, or different from, Herriot's description of the horse's reaction to the injections? How does each display the main features of an observation?

2. Turn back to "Ollie and Ginny: Two Kittens Who Came to Stay." Reread the passages about Herriot's treatment of the kittens' illness. Write a description of Herriot's use of vivid, precise words to recreate events for the reader.

◆ Drawing Conclusions About Herriot's Work

No one was more surprised by his international fame than Herriot himself. The contrast between his careers as a humble country vet and as a best-selling author is extreme. But in many ways it is precisely his modesty and good humor that led to his runaway success as an author.

Another reason for the strong appeal of Herriot's stories is their emotional pull. Many readers share Herriot's strong feelings about animals. As they read his descriptions of animals in sickness and health, they feel a powerful emotional response.

Write a paragraph in which you choose one of Herriot's stories and identify the details that appeal to the reader's emotions. You can begin by listing particular words or phrases Herriot uses to achieve this effect.

◆ Idea Bank

Writing

1. **Clinic Notes** Veterinarians often keep records of their patients' illnesses and health. Choose one of the animals that Herriot treats in these stories. Summarize the animal's illness, treatment, and results in the form of medical notes. Use headings such as "type of animal," "general condition," "symptoms," "diagnosis," "treatment," and "outcome."

2. **Compare and Contrast** Write a paragraph in which you compare Olly and Ginny with a pet you have known. Describe how these cats were similar to and different from the pet. Be sure to include a full description of each animal you discuss.

3. **Retelling** Write a short story in which you retell one of Herriot's stories from a different point of view. You might choose one of the human or animal characters as a narrator. Review the original story for basic plot elements. Then try to imagine how your character might have perceived the events differently.

Speaking, Listening, and Viewing

4. **Interview** Imagine that James Herriot is coming to your school. Work with a group to create a list of questions you could ask the author about his writing and about his career as a vet. Take turns playing the role of Herriot and asking questions. Discuss whether or not the responses seem realistic and in keeping with Herriot's personality. **[Performing Arts Link; Group Activity]**

Researching and Representing

5. **Career Report** Find out what kind of training is required to become a veterinarian. Create a timeline or schedule that shows how long each educational stage takes. Include information about the kinds of coursework, examinations, and training veterinary students must complete. **[Career Link]**

6. **Multimedia Story** Create a multimedia presentation about a veterinarian in your community. You can include interviews with the vet as well as with people who bring their pets to his or her office. Your presentation could also include photographs, audio or video recordings, and artwork.

◆ Further Reading, Listening, and Viewing

- Lord, Graham. *James Herriot: The Life of a Country Vet* (1997). This detailed biography describes the key events in Herriot's surprising life.
- Wight, Jim. *The Real James Herriot: A Memoir of My Father* (2000). Herriot's son, who also became a veterinarian, shares his warm memories of his father.
- *James Herriot's Yorkshire Revisited* (1999) and *James Herriot's Yorkshire*. This book and the related documentary video take viewers on a tour of the Yorkshire countryside that inspired Herriot.

On the Web:

http://www.phschool.com/atschool/literature
Go to the student edition *Bronze*. Proceed to Unit 5. Then click Hot Links to find Web sites featuring James Herriot.

Cynthia Rylant In Depth

> "I get a lot of personal gratification thinking of those people who don't get any attention in the world and making them really valuable in my fiction—making them absolutely shine with their beauty."
>
> — *Cynthia Rylant*

CYNTHIA RYLANT has written dozens of books for children and young adults, including picture books, short stories, novels, poetry, biography, and autobiography. With great warmth and a down-to-earth sense of humor, she explores the hopes and dreams, joys and losses of ordinary people, especially those of Appalachia, where she grew up. Her subjects cover a broad range—family life, animals, the choices that young people must make, and the challenges faced by older people.

Childhood Losses, Childhood Joys

Cynthia Rylant was born on June 6, 1954, in Hopewell, Virginia. When she was four years old, Cynthia and her mother moved to West Virginia, where Cynthia's grandparents cared for her for several years while her mother was away at nursing school.

Though she missed her mother deeply, a large and loving network of extended family, friends, and neighbors in her small rural community surrounded Rylant. She has many happy memories of her childhood, despite the family's poverty.

As a girl, Rylant loved to wander the back roads of her town—exploring, dreaming, making friends with all the local dogs, and observing the daily life of her friends and neighbors. She recalls being a sensitive child who "grieved over stray animals," and loved solitude as much as she loved having friends.

Youthful Dreams As she grew into her teens, Rylant began to feel restless in her small community and longed for broader horizons. Because the town had no library or bookstore, for example, Rylant became a regular consumer of comic books. Although she loved the people and the beautiful countryside, she began to dream of joining a larger world of musicians, artists, and writers.

In her autobiography *But I'll Be Back Again,* Rylant remembers two events from her teen years that expanded her awareness of the larger world. One was Senator Robert F. Kennedy's visit to her hometown in 1968, during his campaign for President. Rylant was in the crowd that met Kennedy at the airport, and she was able to shake his hand. Kennedy became a personal hero for her, and she was deeply troubled by his assassination just months later.

The other transforming event was a concert given in her school gymnasium by a traveling symphony orchestra. Rylant had never heard classical music before, and she was stunned by the performance. As she watched, she wondered what it would be like to spend one's life creating something so beautiful.

Becoming a Writer When Rylant left home for college in the 1970's, her life began to change dramatically. Her college English classes were a joyful discovery; she particularly remembers being "knocked off (her) feet" by a Langston Hughes story. She went on to earn a Master's degree in English Literature.

After college, she worked in the children's room of a public library, where she discovered great children's books for the first time. Inspired, she wrote her first book, *When I Was Young in the Mountains,* as a tribute to her grandparents, and the book was an immediate success, recognized as a Caldecott Honor Book in 1983.

Growing Success Cynthia Rylant soon became a critically acclaimed author of more books, including *The Relatives Came,* as well as the first volume in the now long-running "Henry and Mudge" series, about a boy and his dog. She branched out into poetry, short stories, and, in 1985, her first novel for young adults, *A Blue-Eyed Daisy.* Her novel *Missing May* won the prestigious Newbery Medal in 1993.

In 1993, Rylant broadened her career further when she began illustrating as well as writing her books. She was inspired to take this leap into art by the paintings of Grandma Moses, an untrained artist who celebrated the joys of rural life. "I felt such a freedom looking at her paintings," Rylant explains.

In recent years, she has experimented with both acrylic paintings and cut-paper collages as a creative outlet. She has illustrated her "Everyday Book" series, as well as *Dog Heaven, The Whales,* and *The Bookshop Dog.*

Dreams Come True As a child, Rylant longed for a nice house, her own dogs and cats, and the opportunity to do something important. Today, she feels that those dreams have come true. The mother of a grown son, Rylant lives in a cozy house with two dogs and two cats. She loves movies, chocolate, stained glass, decorating her house, and writing.

Cynthia Rylant is a writer with a unique voice and a deep sensitivity to the struggles and joys of everyday life. She is drawn to characters of all ages who live their lives with quiet dignity. She believes that "the best writing is that which is most personal, most revealing."

◆ Humane Treatment of Animals

Cynthia Rylant's characters form strong attachments with animals and struggle to protect and nurture them. Rylant herself shares this connection with animals. Though she enjoys the solitude of writing, she couldn't imagine living without the companionship of her two dogs.

Many Americans share Rylant's concern for animals. The first organization formed to protect animals in the United States was the American Society for the Prevention of Cruelty to Animals (ASPCA), founded in the state of New York in 1866. Today, there are many similar organizations throughout the nation. These groups work to educate the public about humane animal care and to enforce state laws protecting animals. They also maintain animal shelters for lost or abandoned pets and oversee the adoption of stray animals.

◆ Literary Works

Novels
- *A Blue-Eyed Daisy* (1985)
- *A Fine White Dust* (1986)
- *Missing May* (1992)

Short Stories
- *Children of Christmas: Stories for the Season* (1987)
- *A Couple of Kooks: And Other Stories About Love* (1990)

Poetry
- *Waiting to Waltz…A Childhood* (1984)
- *Soda Jerk* (1990)

Nonfiction
- *But I'll Be Back Again: An Album* (1989)
- *Appalachia: The Voices of Sleeping Birds* (1991)
- *Margaret, Frank, and Andy* (1996)

Cynthia Rylant

Halfway Home

Her father is ordering eggs and toast as he warms his hands over his coffee cup. Frances wants only a piece of cherry pie. And hot chocolate. The diner is steamy with the aroma of fried potatoes and hamburger grease, and its foggy windows hide the snow outside.

It is, for Frances, like a long, skinny, smelly cocoon this Christmas Eve. She is wrapped with her father into this safe, warm place.

They have just picked up the sewing machine for her mother, and Frances thinks of it in its box in the trunk of the car. The machine is black, with gold designs. It is very elegant. Her mother will love them for buying it.

It is already dark outside. Frances is usually home at this time on Christmas Eve. But the drive to the city was long, and so many cars, and waiting in line at the sewing machine store. She and her father are only halfway home now. Maybe they should have kept driving. But they were so hungry . . .

Frances watches the waitress fry her father's eggs. the woman has a round sun face and dove eyes and her long blonde hair is pulled back tight, running to her waist. Frances watches her and wonders if she will fry eggs here all night, and if someone will have a surprise present for her on Christmas morning.

Only four people are eating in this diner this Christmas Eve. Frances, her father, a big man in a plaid coat, and a thin young man with a beard. The young man has a paperback book in his left hand, and he reads it while he spoons chili into his mouth with his right. The big man just stares at nothing while he drinks his coffee.

When the waitress sets the food they ordered in front of Frances and her father, she smiles at Frances and squirts a giant dollop[1] of whipped cream atop the hot chocolate. It's the most whipped cream Frances has ever had on hot chocolate and her eyes are very big.

Christmas music plays on the diner's radio, hot coffee brews, and the five people in the cocoon are quiet with their thoughts and their hunger this night.

Suddenly, Frances sees a shadow at one of the diner's windows. She looks hard. The shadow has a tail.

---

1. dollop (dŏl′ əp): A soft mass or blob, as of food.

"Daddy, look. A cat!"

Frances' father and the waitress and the big man and the young man all turn to the window where Frances is pointing. The shadow's tail moves back and forth on the foggy glass.

Everyone in the diner looks at everyone else for a moment. They look back at the window. They look at each other again. Finally, the waitress comes from behind the counter and opens the door.

"Here, kitty," she calls.

And quicker than any expects, the shadow with a tail is gone and a black cat is walking in the door.

The cat is long and skinny, like the diner, and the top of its head is sprinkled with snowflakes. Its large green eyes look directly into the eyes of the waitress, then, rubbing against her legs, the cat squeaks out a meow.

"Goodness sakes," says the waitress.

The big man in the plaid coat says it first:

"Looks hungry."

Frances looks at her father's plate full of eggs, then she looks at her father. He gives her a What-do-you-mean-give-that-cat-my-eggs? look.

The sun-faced waitress scoops the cat up in her arms. She says to everybody in the diner, "This cat's not supposed to be here, you know."

Everybody nods his head.

"Against health regulations," she says, scratching the cat behind its ear.

Everybody nods again. No one speaks. Then the young man says, "You think it'll eat chili?"

He holds his bowl out to the waitress.

Everybody laughs then and they all say something about it being Christmas and what kind of regulations would keep a hungry cat outside, and the waitress is setting the cat back on the floor again, offering it the warm safety of her diner.

Frances jumps off her stool and goes to the cat. They all watch as the cat rubs against her, pushing its nose into her hair. Frances' father lets his eggs get cold as he watches her with bright eyes.

When the waitress puts a saucer of milk on the counter, Frances lifts the cat up. Everyone watches the animal drink deep and long, and the big man says "About starved" and the young man says "Pretty animal" and the waitress says "Poor thing."

After drinking the milk, the cat walks up and down the length of the counter, stepping over salt and pepper shakers, circling coffee cups, to say hello to everyone. The waitress, who is frying a hamburger for the animal, looks alarmed at first, but the diner's customers are all smiling and laughing and reaching out to touch the soft black fur. She lets the cat walk.

Finally the big man says, "Well, who's going to take it home?"

Everyone except Frances shrugs his shoulders and watches the cat eat the little pieces of hamburger the waitress has crumbled up on a plate.

"Daddy?" Frances says.

Her father shakes his head.

"Can't," he says.

Frances sighs and looks at the other people. She can't imagine the cat with any of them. She can imagine it only with her.

"Maybe he belongs around here," says the young man.

"I've never seen him before," the waitress answers.

"Pretty thing," says the young man. His paperback book is lying closed beside his chili bowl.

"My wife would skin me[2] if I brought some creature in on Christmas Eve," the big man admits to everyone who is listening.

Frances' father nods his head.

"Mine, too," he says.

Frances raises her eyebrows and looks at him, shocked. But she doesn't know why she's shocked. What he says is probably true.

She waits for the young man or the waitress to tell who is waiting at home for them this Christmas Eve, who will skin them if they bring a creature home.

But neither speaks.

"Daddy, the waitress won't put him back outside, will she?" Frances asks her father.

"I don't know, dear."

Frances wants to know what will happen to this cat.

"At least he's fed, Frances," her father adds, taking the last drink of his coffee. "Let's hurry and get on the road."

Frances tries finishing the cherry pie, but she hasn't much appetite now. She thinks she might cry.

The big man in plaid gets up and pays for his meal, then he is gone, wishing everybody a merry Christmas as he heads out the door.

And the black cat is sleepy now. It curls itself up on a newspaper beside the cash register, its purring hard and heavy.

Humming, the waitress wipes off the countertop while the young man watches her and watches the cat.

"Looks like he's found a home," the young man says.

The waitress smiles and shakes her head.

"I don't know," she answers. "I'm not looking for a cat on Christmas Eve."

---

2. **"My wife would skin me . . .":** My wife would be very angry with me.

The young man shakes his head, too.

"Neither am I."

He is staring into his cold bowl of chili.

"How long are you open tonight?" he asks.

The waitress smiles again.

"Till I get tired of it, I guess."

"Let's go, Frances," says Frances' father.

While he is paying for their food, Frances is standing at the door.

She looks at the young man sitting alone at the counter, his chili cold, his book unread.

She looks at the sun-faced waitress standing at the cash register, her face moist and clear from the heat of the grill.

She looks at the black cat, its back moving up and down in long deep breathing, lying in peace on the counter.

She follows her father through the door, but as she steps outside, Frances looks back inside one more time. The young man has moved now beside the cat and he is stroking its dark fur. The waitress is talking to him and smiling as she pours him another cup of coffee. The windows are beginning to frost, hiding outside shadows. The smell of fried potatoes lingers in the air. And "Silent Night" is playing on the radio.

Frances smiles at her father, and they start for home.

☑ Check Your Comprehension

1. When and where does the story take place?
2. Summarize how the characters in the story respond when the stray cat arrives.
3. Why won't Frances's father let her bring the cat home?
4. Describe what Frances sees at the end of the story, just before she and her father resume their journey home.

◆ Critical Thinking

INTERPRET

1. Do you think that all of the characters in the story like animals? Support your answer with evidence from the story. **[Infer]**

2. Were you surprised that Frances's father would not let her keep the cat? Why or why not? **[Connect]**
3. Do you think the cat will find a home? Use details from the story to support your answer. **[Speculate]**

EVALUATE

4. Is "Halfway Home" a good title for this story? Why or why not? **[Evaluate]**

APPLY

5. Think of a time when you wanted something you could not have. Compare your own reaction in this situation to Frances's reaction. **[Relate]**

Cynthia Rylant

Planting Things

$\mathbf{M}$r. Willis was a man who enjoyed planting things. He had several beds of zinnias,[1] a large circle of green onions, a couple of barrels of eggplants, a row of spinach and some Swedish ivy on his front porch. Mr. Willis was not a practical gardener, so it did not matter to him whether or not he could eat what he grew, or even if what he planted grew badly or not at all. Mr. Willis just enjoyed planting things.

Mr. Willis's wife lived with him and she was not well. She was old (as was he, but it didn't seem to bother him so much), and she lay in bed most of every day. Mr. Willis loved her—he had loved her for fifty-six years—and he tended to her needs. Her favorite food was a chocolate milkshake mixed up with an egg and some powdered malt. He fixed one for her twice a day—and more, if she asked.

Mr. Willis missed his wife as he puttered about his yard, planting his favorite things. Sometimes she would pull herself up from her bed and stand at the window, watching him work among his onions or zinnias. But not often. She did not seem to enjoy life any longer since she had become old, as if she had decided there was no more for her to do. And Mr. Willis, as hard a he might try, could not change this.

On summer evenings, if the mosquitoes weren't too bad, Mr. Willis sat on his front porch and listened to the sound of children playing at the house just down the road. Traffic was light, and he could hear the crickets and the katydids in his apple trees. Sometimes he almost forgot, sitting there, that Mrs. Willis was in the house.

On his porch, Mr. Willis's Swedish ivy, growing down from a pot attached to the ceiling, was so healthy that Mr. Willis did not tend to it as he did his other growing things. Plucking off a brown leaf or two, that was all the plant required, and Mr. Willis could ignore it for days.

But on one summer evening, when there was still light enough outside to show up a brown leaf for plucking, Mr. Willis's Swedish ivy gave him the surprise of his life.

On top of the pot, among the ivy, a robin had built her nest. Right there, on the porch of Mr. Henry P. Willis, she had nested. There were plenty of trees about, but no, she had chosen to grow her babies on his porch.

---

1. **zinnias** (zin´ ē əz): Large, brightly colored flowers.

Mr. Willis had thought at first she was one of those stuffed birds used to decorate Christmas trees or Easter bonnets. He thought someone had tricked him.

Still, being a cautious man, he had not reached for the bird but had moved closer, eye-level with her. And he knew then she was real. Real and sitting on eggs.

"Charlotte!" He went right to his wife's bedroom. "Charlotte!"

She was lying on her back, looking up at the ceiling. The room was gray.

"Charlotte, you will never believe this. There is a bird nesting in the Swedish ivy!" Mr. Willis's face was the brightest object in the room. She could see it shining. He took hold of her hand.

"It's a robin, dear," he said. "A *robin*. And she has eggs. I stood right beside her—can you believe it!"

Mrs. Willis smiled slightly.

"I'm happy for you, dear," she said.

Mr. Willis rubbed the top of her hand.

"Would you like to see?" he asked.

"I don't think so right now."

So Mr. Willis went back out to the porch, quietly closing the door behind him, and he sat down softly in his chair and watched the bird, feeling his heart pound in his chest.

The following morning Mr. Willis went to check the nest. The bird was away, and he saw three blue eggs lying in the nest, Swedish ivy bunched all around and spilling from the pot. Mr. Willis knew not to touch the eggs. He went on to his chores and waited for the robin to return.

After he had given his wife her morning milkshake, he asked her again, gently propping up the pillows behind her head, "Would you like to see the nest, dear?"

Mrs. Willis smiled and patted his hand. "I'll see it. Don't worry. I'll see it soon."

"Would you like to see it now? Can I help you out to the porch?"

Mrs. Willis sighed. "No, thank you, dear. I'll just lie here and rest a while. You go on. Don't worry about me."

Mr. Willis left her, worrying about her as he did nearly every minute he was awake. He pulled up some onions, watered the eggplant and checked the nest again.

The robin was back, sitting like a statue, never moving her head or blinking an eye, no matter how near Mr. Willis stood. Her being there on his porch among his ivy took his breath away.

One day Mrs. Willis stood at the front door and finally did see the bird, to satisfy her husband. She said she found the bird's being there "curious" and went back to bed.

Mr. Willis spent many summer evenings sitting on the porch with the robin. He never told anyone else about her, never pointed her out to visitors, for he feared that someone might frighten her or touch her eggs or steal her nest. He had learned that she would not leave her nest to protect herself.

Sitting with her, day after day, was like waiting for a baby to be born, as it had been for Mr. and Mrs. Willis when they were young and expecting their child. It had been quiet then, too, the waiting. The world had slowed down for them, and the days had been long and full of conversation. And finally their baby boy Tom had come.

Mr. Willis remembered this, sitting with the robin, and it gave him a feeling of great peace. He was sorry he and his wife had had only one child.

All three of the robin's eggs hatched sometime on a Thursday morning. Mr. Willis went to check on the nest after fixing his wife's breakfast, and he discovered the robin missing and three skinny, squawking babies.

"Well!" he said to them. "I'm a daddy!" He stood beside the nest, beaming.

In the days that followed, the mother robin was away from the nest most of the time, hunting for food. Mr. Willis wished he could make it easier for her—and he tried leaving popcorn and bread on the porch—but she was a particular mother and seemed to want only baby food he could not supply.

So he just sat with her babies, commending² them on their fine growing bodies and scolding them for their constantly gaping mouths.

He sat in his chair and watched the birds and laughed out loud.

Mrs. Willis stood at the door once, watching her husband and his birds. She was surprised they had actually hatched, and she congratulated him.

"You have always done well with your planting, dear," she said. "Your Swedish ivy must have been good for them."

Then she went back to bed.

Mr. Willis had thought the birds would probably fly away from the nest one by one, as children do.

But one day, they were all gone, the mother and the children, and they did not come back.

It is probably best, thought Mr. Willis. Best they go all at once, with no long leave-takings and teary good-byes again and again.

But he did not miss them any the less, just because they had all flown in one morning. The empty nest stayed in the ivy until

---

2. **commending** (kə mend´ ing): Praising; congratulating.

the winter, when he was sure they wouldn't be back.

He brought his chair and his ivy inside for the season, removing the nest and putting it on top of his dresser.

Mr. Willis would look after his wife all winter. Then, come spring, he would put the nest, ready-made, in one of his apple trees.

He was a man who enjoyed planting things.

☑ **Check Your Comprehension**

1. How have Mr. Willis and Mrs. Willis reacted differently to the process of growing older?

2. What does Mr. Willis find in the pot of Swedish ivy on his porch?

3. How does Mrs. Willis respond to her husband's discovery?

4. What does Mr. Willis wait for on his front porch for many days? Of what does the waiting remind him?

5. At the end of the story, what plan does Mr. Willis have for the spring?

◆ **Critical Thinking**

INTERPRET

1. What effect does the surprise in his Swedish ivy have on Mr. Willis? **[Analyze Cause and Effect]**

2. Why does Mr. Willis try so hard to interest his wife in the surprise? **[Draw Conclusions]**

COMPARE LITERARY WORKS

3. How does the presence of animals affect the characters in "Planting Things" and "Halfway Home"? **[Connect]**

EVALUATE

4. How would the story's tone be different if Mr. Willis had succeeded in engaging his wife's interest in the bird? **[Evaluate]**

APPLY

5. In your experience, how easy or difficult is it for one person to change another person's attitude toward life? Explain your answer. **[Relate]**

ynthia Rylant

A Bad Road for Cats

"Louie! Louis! Where are you?"

The woman called it out again and again as she walked along Route 6. A bad road for cats. She prayed he hadn't wandered this far. But it had been nearly two weeks, and still Louis hadn't come home.

She stopped at a Shell station, striding up to the young man at the register. Her eyes snapped black and fiery as she spit the question at him:

"Have you seen a *cat?*" The word *cat* came out hard as a rock.

The young man straightened up.

"No, ma'am. No cats around here. Somebody dropped a mutt off a couple nights ago, but a Mack truck got it yesterday about noon. Dog didn't have a chance."

The woman's eyes pinched his.

"I lost my cat. Orange and white. If you see him, you be more careful of him than that dog. This is a bad road for cats."

She marked toward the door.

"I'll be back," she said, like a threat, and the young man straightened up again as she went out.

"Louie! Louis! Where are you?"

She was a very tall woman, and skinny. Her black hair was long and shiny, like an Indian's. She might have been a Cherokee making her way alongside a river, alert and watchful. Tracking.

But Route 6 was no river. It was a truckers' road, lined with gas stations, motels, dairy bars, diners. A nasty road, smelling of diesel[1] and rubber.

The woman's name was Magda. And she was of French blood, not Indian. Magda was not old, but she carried herself as a very old and strong person might, with no fear of death and with a clear sense of her right to the earth and a disdain[2] for the ugliness of belching machines and concrete.

Magda lived in a small house about two miles off Route 6. There she worked at a loom, weaving wool gathered from the sheep she owned. Magda's husband was dead, and she had no children. Only a cat named Louis.

Dunh. Dunh. Duuunnh.

Magda's heart pounded as a tank truck roared by. *Duuunnh.*

---

1. diesel: (dēz´ əl): Special fuel used by big trucks.
2. disdain: Scorn; contempt.

The horn hurt her ears, making her feel sick inside, stealing some of her strength.

Four years before, Magda had found Louis at one of the gas stations on Route 6. She had been on her way home from her weekly trip to the grocery and had pulled in for a fill-up. As she'd stood inside the station, she'd felt warm fur against her leg and had given a start.[3] Looking down, she'd seen an orange-and-white kitten. It had purred and meowed and pushed its nose into Magda's shoes. Smiling, Magda had picked the kitten up. Then she had seen the horror.

Half of the kitten's tail was gone. What remained was bloody and scabbed, and the stump stuck straight out.

Magda had carried the animal to one of the station attendants.

"Whose kitten is this?" Her eyes drilled in the question.

The attendant had shrugged his shoulders.

"Nobody's. Just a drop-off."

Magda had moved closer to him.

"What happened to its *tail*?" she asked, the words slow and clear.

"Got caught in the door. Stupid cat was under everybody's feet—no wonder half its tail got whacked."

Magda could not believe such a thing.

"And you offer it no *help*?" she had asked.

"Not my cat," he answered.

Magda's face had blazed as she'd turned and stalked out the door with the kitten.

A veterinarian mended what was left of the kitten's tail. And Magda named it Louis for her grandfather.

"Louie! Louis! Where are you?"

Dunh. Duuunnh. Another horn at her back. Magda wondered about her decision to walk Route 6 rather than drive it. She had thought that on foot she might find Louis more easily—in a ditch, under some bushes, up a tree. They were even, she and Louis, if she were on foot, too. But the trucks were making her misery worse.

Magda saw a dairy bar up ahead. She thought she would stop and rest. She would have some coffee and a slice of quiet away from the road.

She walked across the wide gravel lot to the tiny walk-up window. Pictures of strawberry sundaes, spongy shakes, cones with curly peaks were plastered all over the building, drawing business from the road with big red words like *CHILLY*.

Magda barely glanced at the young girl working inside. All teenage girls looked alike to her.

---

3. **given a start:** Jumped suddenly in surprise.

"Coffee," she ordered.

"Black?"

"Yes."

Magda moved to one side and leaned against the building. The trucks were rolling out on the highway, but far enough away to give her time to regain her strength. No horns, no smoke, no dirt. A little peace.

She drank her coffee and thought about Louis when he was a kitten. Once, he had leaped from her attic window and she had found him, stunned and shivering, on the hard gravel below. The veterinarian said Louis had broken a leg and was lucky to be alive. The kitten had stomped around in a cast for a few weeks. Magda drew funny faces on it to cheer him up.

Louis loved white cheese, tall grass and the skeins of wool Magda left lying around her loom.

That's what she would miss most, she thought, if Louis never came back: an orange and white cat making the yarn fly under her loom.

Magda finished her coffee, then turned to throw the empty cup in the trash can. As she did, a little sign in the bottom corner of the window caught her eye. The words were surrounded by dirty smudges:

4 Sal. CAT

Magda caught her breath. She moved up to the window and this time looked squarely into the face of the girl.

"Are you selling a *cat*?" she said quietly, but hard on *cat.* "Not me. This boy," the girl answered, brushing her stringy hair back from her face.

"Where is he?" Magda asked.

"That yellow house right off the road up there."

Magda headed across the lot.

She had to knock only once. The door opened and standing there was a boy about fifteen.

"I saw your sign," Magda said. "I am interested in your cat."

The boy did not answer. He looked at Magda's face with his wide blue eyes, and he grinned, showing a mouth of rotten and missing teeth.

Magda felt a chill move over her.

"The cat," she repeated. "You have one to sell? Is it orange and white?"

The boy stopped grinning. Without a word, he slammed the door in Magda's face.

She was stunned. A strong woman like her, to be so stunned by a boy. It shamed her. But again she knocked on the door— and very hard this time.

No answer.

What kind of boy is this? Magda asked herself. A strange one. And she feared he had Louis.

She had just raised her hand to knock a third time when the door opened. There the boy stood with Louis in his arms.

Again, Magda was stunned. Her cat was covered with oil and dirt. He was thin, and his head hung weakly. When he saw Magda, he seemed to use his last bit of strength to let go a pleading cry.

The boy no longer was grinning. He held Louis close against him, forcefully stroking the cat's ears again and again and again. The boy's eyes were full of tears, his mouth twisted into sad protest.

Magda wanted to leap for Louis, steal him and run for home. But she knew better. This was an unusual boy. She must be careful.

Magda put her hand into her pocket and pulled out a dollar bill.

"Enough?" she asked, holding it up.

The boy clutched the cat harder, his mouth puckering fiercely.

Magda pulled out two more dollar bills. She held the money up, the question in her eyes.

The boy relaxed his hold on Louis. He tilted his head to one side, as if considering Magda's offer.

Then, in desperation, Magda pulled out a twenty-dollar bill.

"Enough?" She almost screamed.

The boy's head jerked upright, then he grabbed all the bills with one hand and shoved Louis at Magda with the other.

Magda cradled Louis in her arms. Rubbing her cheek across his head. Before walking away, she looked once more at the boy. He stood stiffly with the money clenched in his hand, tears running from his eyes and dripping off his face like rainwater.

Magda took Louis home. She washed him and healed him. And for many days she was in a rage at the strange boy who had sold her her own cat, nearly dead.

When Louis was healthy, though, and his old fat self, playing games among the yarn beneath her loom, her rage grew smaller and smaller until finally she could forgive the strange boy.

She came to feel sympathy for him, remembering his tears. And she wove some orange and white wool into a pattern, stuffed it with cotton, sewed two green button eyes and small pink mouth onto it, then attached a matching stub of a tail.

She put the gift in a paper bag, and, on her way to the grocery one day, she dropped the bag in front of the boy's yellow house.

☑ Check Your Comprehension

1. At the beginning of the story, how long has Magda's cat, Louis, been missing?
2. Briefly summarize how Magda came to own Louis.
3. Explain how Magda eventually finds Louis.
4. Describe the boy who has been keeping Louis and how the boy reacts when Magda comes for the cat.
5. How do Magda's feelings for the boy change after she takes Louis home? In the end, how does she express her feelings for the boy?

◆ Critical Thinking

INTERPRET

1. How does Rylant make Magda a distinctive character? How is she different from the two gas station attendants, for example? **[Compare and Contrast]**

2. Why do you think the boy took Magda's cat? Use details from the story to support your answer. **[Infer]**
3. Why do you think the boy makes Magda pay so much money to get her cat back? **[Draw Conclusions]**

EVALUATE

4. Do you think that Magda should have let the boy keep Louis? Why or why not? **[Make a Judgment]**

EXTEND

5. Do you think that people should be made legally responsible for abandoning a pet? What alternatives do pet owners have when they cannot, or no longer wish to, care for a pet? **[Social Studies Link]**

Cynthia Rylant
Comparing and Connecting the Author's Works

◆ **Literary Focus: Direct and Indirect Characterization**

In Cynthia Rylant's stories, readers come to understand a broad range of characters. The technique authors use to portray a character is called **characterization**. There are two ways that authors reveal a character's personality: with the characters' own words, thoughts, and actions and by describing their interactions with other characters. It is then up to the reader to examine all these clues and decide what the character is like.

In "Planting Things," for example, Rylant reveals Mr. Willis's character more deeply by describing his thoughts, feelings, words, and actions after he discovers the robin's nest on his porch. For example, when Mr. Wills first finds the nest, he rushes to tell his wife the news, and his face lights up so much that it is "the brightest object in the room." Later, as he watches the mother robin, he can feel his heart pounding in his chest with excitement. From these clues, the reader can tell that Mr. Willis is a man who loves animals and new life, who delights in the small miracles of nature, and who yearns to share his joy with his wife.

1. Describe the character of Mrs. Willis in "Planting Things." Support your answer using details of her thoughts, words, and actions.

2. In "Halfway Home" Rylant uses characterization to reveal the personalities of the five characters in the diner. Choose one of the characters. Find examples of what the character says, does, or thinks in the story. Then use these clues to describe the character's personality.

◆ **Drawing Conclusions about Rylant's Work**

One critic has written that Cynthia Rylant's stories "explore deep feelings of love, belonging, and loss." Another critic emphasizes the feeling of hope conveyed in Rylant's work: "Despite the inclusion of such themes as loneliness, fear, or betrayal, her works ultimately convey understanding and hope."

Each of the main characters in the three stories you have read experiences loss and loneliness and later find reasons for hope. Mr. Willis in "Planting Things," for example, feels lonely because he feels he has lost his wife's companionship. He finds a sense of connection and hope, however, as he watches the hatching of the baby robins on his porch.

Complete the diagram below by filling in details about the main characters in "Planting Things" and "A Bad Road for Cats."

	Character feels loss and loneliness because . . .	Character finds hope because . . .
MAGDA		
MR. WILLIS		

◆ Idea Bank

Writing

1. **Personal Memoir** Write your own true story about how a relationship with an animal has changed your life or the life of someone you know.

2. **Letter** Write a letter to Cynthia Rylant explaining what you liked or disliked about one of her stories. Mention specific characters and events from the story in your letter.

3. **Compare and Contrast Characters** Write a one-page essay exploring the similarities and differences between two characters in the same story or two characters from different stories by Rylant. Before you begin writing, make a Venn diagram detailing the characters' differences and similarities.

Speaking and Listening

4. **Dramatic Presentation** Working with a partner or a small group, choose a scene from one of Rylant's stories to present as a play. Prepare a script, choose individual parts, and rehearse. Then present the scene to the class. **[Performing Arts Link]**

Researching and Representing

5. **Portrait** Reread one of Rylant's stories and try to imagine the physical appearance of the main character and the animal that touches the character's life. Then draw a portrait of the main character and the animal together.

6. **Poster** Visit your local Humane Society or Society for the Prevention of Cruelty to Animals. Pick up brochures that describe the services offered by the organization, and arrange to tour the facilities and interview a staff member. Then make a poster advertising the organization's services or urging people to "adopt" strays from a local animal shelter.

◆ Further Reading, Listening, and Viewing

- Cynthia Rylant: *When I Was Young in the Mountains* (1982). In her first published book, Rylant recalls life in the Appalachian Mountains. Praised for its simple, evocative language, this picture book has received numerous awards.

- Cynthia Rylant: *Every Living Thing* (1985). This award-winning collection includes tales of how people's lives are enriched through their relationships with animals.

- Cynthia Rylant: *Best Wishes* (1992). In this short autobiography, illustrated with photos, the author describes her childhood dreams and how she was able to fulfill them.

- Cynthia Rylant: *Missing May* (1995). Audio-cassette. You can listen to the audio version of Rylant's Newbery Award-winning novel about love, death, grief, and hope.

- *Cynthia Rylant* (VHS). This video addresses Rylant's childhood in Appalachia and her path to success as an award-winning author.

On the Web:

http://www.phschool.com/atschool/literature
Go to the student edition *Bronze*. Proceed to Unit 6. Then click Hot Links to find Web sites featuring Cynthia Rylant.

Marjorie Kinnan Rawlings In Depth

"We need above all, I think, a certain remoteness from urban confusion, and while this can be found in other places, Cross Creek offers it with such beauty and grace that once entangled with it, no other place seems possible…"

— *Marjorie Kinnan Rawlings*

MARJORIE KINNAN RAWLINGS saw beauty and inspiration in the lives of poor farmers struggling to survive in an often harsh wilderness. By vividly describing the realities of living close to nature, she affirmed the fundamental values that, for her, made life worth living. Her novel *The Yearling* won her the Pulitzer Prize in 1939.

Off to an Early Start Marjorie Kinnan Rawlings was born on August 8, 1896, in Washington, D.C., where her father worked. From an early age, Rawlings loved to write, and her mother encouraged her to submit her work to the children's pages of local newspapers. At the age of eleven, she won a prize for a story published in the *Washington Post,* and at sixteen she won second place in a writing contest sponsored by *McCall's* magazine.

Rawlings also discovered her love of the country at an early age. Her father owned a farm in Maryland, where the family spent the summers living in tents, and where Rawlings and her brother spent their days hiking and fishing. Later, she would remember these summers in the country as her happiest childhood memories.

Tragedy and Moving On In 1914, Rawlings' father died just as she was to graduate from high school. Her mother decided to move the family to Madison, Wisconsin, to be near family friends. There, Rawlings attended the University of Wisconsin, where she majored in English and wrote for the campus literary magazine.

Struggle and Disappointment After her graduation from college in 1918, Rawlings moved to New York City, where she dreamed of finding success as a writer. In 1919 she married Charles Rawlings, a college classmate who also dreamed of being a writer. Rawlings and her husband both found jobs at a newspaper in Rochester, New York, where for years Rawlings was assigned to write feature stories and light poetry intended for women readers. Eventually, she came to dislike this job and to grow tired of city life.

Escape to Cross Creek Rawlings and her husband decided to buy an orange grove in Cross Creek, Florida, in 1928. Their life in Florida was not the romantic dream they had imagined. Despite her disappointment, however, Rawlings stayed on at Cross Creek. She had found peace in its harsh, but beautiful, natural environment. She had also discovered the setting and characters that would her inspire her best writing.

Home at Last Rawlings felt instantly at home among the lakes, marshes, pine trees, and orange groves of Cross Creek's "scrub country." She immediately began to keep a journal of her impressions, describing the native plants and animals, her hard work in the orange grove, and the dialect and traditional customs of her neighbors. A year after her arrival in Cross Creek, Rawlings began publishing her observations as a series of magazine articles.

Going Deeper Rawlings' articles caught the attention of Maxwell Perkins, an important book editor in New York City, who wrote to her, suggesting that she use her observations as the basis for a novel. Her first novel, *South Moon Under*, published in 1933, won glowing reviews for its rich description of a way of life new to American literature.

An American Classic By 1936 Rawlings was ready to start working on a novel about a young boy, based on an idea that Perkins had suggested to her. The result was *The Yearling*, published in 1938. It tells the story of a lonely boy from a desperately poor family who deeply loves the orphaned fawn he has rescued. *The Yearling* won a Pulitzer Prize in 1939. It went on to become an American classic.

Financial Success and National Celebrity *The Yearling* was a bestseller. It brought Rawlings the first financial success she had ever known and made her famous. After its publication, she met fellow novelists Ernest Hemingway and F. Scott Fitzgerald and became friends with poet Robert Frost. She was even invited to the White House to have lunch with First Lady Eleanor Roosevelt.

After the excitement died down, Rawlings was ready to begin work on a book she had been planning for ten years, a book of autobiographical stories and essays called *Cross Creek*, which was published in 1942.

Leaving Cross Creek In 1941 Rawlings moved to St. Augustine, Florida, but could not adjust to city life. She missed Cross Creek, and she found it increasingly difficult to write without the daily inspiration of her special place. She struggled for ten years to complete her last novel, *The Sojourner*, which was finally published in 1953, just months before her death. Rawlings died unexpectedly on December 14, 1953. She was buried a few miles away from her beloved Cross Creek. Today, her homestead in Cross Creek is a state historic site.

◆ The Florida of Marjorie Kinnan Rawlings

Today, most people think of Florida as a tropical paradise full of beach resorts and theme parks, but this was not the Florida that Marjorie Kinnan Rawlings came to in 1928. Before the 1920's, much of Florida was wilderness, and even after the Great Florida Land Boom of the 1920's, most of northern Florida remained wilderness. Wealthy tourists and developers by-passed this marshy scrub country to reach the tropical southern beaches of Miami, Palm Beach, and Tampa.

Further, the Great Depression of 1929 hit at the same time that the orange groves of Florida were infested by a deadly invasion of Mediterranean fruit flies that destroyed much of the citrus crop. It was not the best time for an inexperienced northerner like Rawlings to try to survive as the new owner of an orange grove. Although Rawlings found personal satisfaction and creative inspiration in Cross Creek, her orange grove was never a financial success.

◆ Literary Works

Fiction
- *South Moon Under* (1933)
- *Golden Apples* (1935)
- *The Yearling* (1938)
- *When the Whippoorwill—* (1940)
- *Jacob's Ladder* (1950)
- *The Sojourner* (1953)

Nonfiction
- *Cross Creek* (1942)
- *Cross Creek Cookery* (1942)

Antses in Tim's Breakfast

I HAVE USED a factual background for most of my tales, and of actual people a blend of the true and the imagined. I myself cannot quite tell where the one ends and the other begins. But I do remember first a place and then a woman, that stabbed me to the core, so that I shall never get over the wound of them.

The place was near the village on the Creek road, and I thought when I saw it that it was a place where children had been playing. A space under a great spreading live oak had been lived in. The sand was trodden smooth and there were a decrepit[1] iron stove and a clothes line, on which a bit of tattered cloth still hung. There were boxes and a rough table, as though little girls had been playing house. Only opened tin cans and a rusty pot, I think, made me inquire about it, for children were not likely to carry a game so far. I was told that a man and woman, very young, had lived there for a part of one summer, coming from none knew where, and going away again with sacks over their shoulders when the autumn frosts came in.

What manner of man and woman could this be, making a home under an oak tree like some pair of woods animals? Were they savage outlaws? People who might more profitably be in jail? I had no way of knowing. The Florida back country was new and beautiful but of the people I knew nothing. The wild home at the edge of the woods haunted me. I made pictures to myself of the man and woman, very young, who had come and gone. Somehow I knew that they would be not fierce, but gentle. I took up my own life at the Creek.

The answer to my wonderings was on my own grove and for a long time I did not know that it was there. A tenant house stood a few hundred yards from my farmhouse. It was placed beautifully under a vast magnolia tree and was all gray age and leaning walls. It was a tall two stories and had perhaps been the original home on the grove. It was windowless and seemed on the point of collapsing within itself. The occupants were Tim and his wife and their baby. I saw only Tim, red-haired and on the defensive[2] and uninterested in his work. His job with the previous owner of the grove had been his first of the kind, he said. His weekly wage was low but I did not question it. He had come with the place. His passion was for trapping and the hides of raccoons and skunks and opossums and an occasional otter or wild-cat hung drying

---

1. decrepit (di krep′ it): Old and broken-down; falling apart.
2. on the defensive: Ready to take offense at the slightest hint of disapproval or criticism.

on the walls of his house. He trapped along the lake edge back of the grove, and I would see him coming in of an early morning with a dead creature or two in his hands. The well at the barn, in front of the tenant house, was sulphurous[3] and fit only for the stock,[4] and Tim came to my pump by my back door for water for his family use. I saw his wife only from a distance and made no inquiries about her.

Callousness, I think, is often ignorance, rather than cruelty, and it was so in my brief relation with Tim and his wife. My excuse is that at the time I myself had so much hard physical work to do and was so confused with the new way of living that I did not understand that life might be much more difficult for others. The woman came striding to my back door one day. She had her baby slung over one hip, like a bundle. She walked with the tread of an Indian, graceful and direct. She was lean and small. As she came close I saw that she had tawny skin and soft honey-colored hair, drawn back smoothly over her ears and knotted at her neck. She held a card in her hand and she thrust it at me.

"Please to read hit," she said.

I took the card, addressed to Tim, and turned it over. It was only an advertisement from a wholesale fur house, quoting current prices on such pelts as Tim trapped for. I must have seemed very stupid to her, for I did not know what she wanted. At last I understood that she could not read, that the card had come in the morning's rural mail while Tim was at work at the far side of the grove. Mail, all reading matter, was cryptic[5] and important and it was necessary to know whether she should call Tim from his work because of the card. I read it aloud and she listened gravely. She took it from me and turned to walk away.

"I thank you," she said.

Her voice was like the note of a thrush, very soft and sweet.

I called after her, seeing her suddenly as a woman, "Tell me, how are you getting on?"

She looked at me with direct gray eyes.

"Nothin' extry. They ain't no screens to the house and the skeeters like to eat us alive. And I cain't keep the antses outen Tim's breakfast."

Her statement was almost unintelligible.[6] I myself was troubled by the mosquitoes, for they came up through holes in the kitchen floor and had my legs swollen to twice their size. But my bedrooms were tight and comfortable, and when sleep is possible, one can stand much in the daytime. I had actually not noticed

---

3. sulphurous: Containing sulfur, or having the "rotten egg" smell characteristic of burning sulfur.
4. stock: Livestock; horses and cows.
5. cryptic: Mysterious; having a hidden meaning.
6. unintelligible (un´ in tel´ i jə bəl): Not able to be understood; incomprehensible.

that the tenant house was wide open to the intrusion not only of insects, but of wind and weather. The matter of ants in the breakfast was beyond me. It was only as I came to know the backwoods cooking customs that I knew that enough food was cooked once or at the most twice a day, to last for the three meals. The people were up long before daylight and remnants of the previous evening's biscuits and greens and fat bacon were set aside for the early breakfast, eaten by lamplight. Where a house was rotting to the ground, ants and roaches inhabited the very wood of floors and walls and swarmed over the family's edibles. The situation of Tim's wife puzzled but still did not concern me. I did not yet understand that in this way of life one is obliged to share, back and forth, and that as long as I had money for screens and a new floor, I was morally obligated to put out a portion of it too give some comfort to those who worked for me. I took others' discomfort for granted and the only palliation[7] of my social sin is that I took my own so, too.

---

7. palliation (pal ē ā´ shən): Excuse; reason that makes an offense less severe.

☑ **Check Your Comprehension**

1. What conclusion does Rawlings first draw when she sees the household items under the live oak tree? Is she correct? Explain.
2. At first, why isn't Rawlings very curious about Tim and his family?
3. What does Tim's wife ask Rawlings to do?
4. Why are there ants in Tim's breakfast?

◆ **Critical Thinking**

INTERPRET

1. Why didn't Rawlings understand that she should help Tim and his wife? **[Analyze Causes and Effects]**

2. Do you think Rawlings would have changed her behavior toward the couple if they had stayed with her longer? **[Speculate]**
3. In your own words, explain why Rawlings is "stabbed . . . to the core" by the memory of Tim's wife. **[Interpret]**

EVALUATE

4. Do you think Rawlings' explanations for her treatment of Tim and his wife are valid? Why or why not? **[Make a Judgment]**

APPLY

5. Rawlings states that callousness is often the result of ignorance rather than cruelty. What do you think the author means by this statement? Of what was Rawlings ignorant? **[Analyze]**

Marjorie Kinnan Rawlings

from The Yearling

JODY opened his eyes unwillingly. Sometime, he thought, he would slip away into the woods and sleep from Friday until Monday. Daylight was showing through the east window of his small bedroom. He could not be certain whether it was the pale light that had awakened him, or the stirring of the chickens in the peach trees. He heard them fluttering one by one from their roost in the branches. The daylight lay in orange streaks. The pines beyond the clearing were still black against it. Now in April the sun was rising earlier. It could not be very late. It was good to awaken by himself before his mother called him. He turned over luxuriously. The dry corn shucks of his mattress rustled under him. The Dominick rooster crowed boisterously under the window.

"You crow now," the boy said. "See kin you rout me out."[1]

The bright streaks in the east thickened and blended. A golden flush spread as high as the pines, and as he watched, the sun itself lifted, like a vast copper skillet being drawn to hang among the branches. A light wind stirred, as though the growing light had pushed it out of the restless east. The sacking[2] curtains eddied[3] out into the room. The breeze reached the bed and brushed him with the cool softness of clean fur. He lay for a moment in torment between the luxury of his bed and the coming day. Then he was out of his nest and standing on the deerskin rug, and his breeches[4] were hanging handily, and his shirt right side out by good fortune, and he was in them, and dressed, and there was not any need of sleep, or anything but the day, and the smell of hot cakes in the kitchen.

"Hey, ol' Ma," he said at the door. "I like you, Ma."

"You and them hounds and all the rest o' the stock," she said. "Mighty lovin' on a empty belly and me with a dish in my hand."

"That's the way you're purtiest," he said, and grinned.

He went whistling to the water-shelf and dipped into the wooden bucket to fill the wash-basin. He soused his hands and face in the water, deciding against the strong lye soap. He wet his hair and parted and smoothed it with his fingers. He took down the small mirror from the wall and studied himself a moment.

"I'm turrible ugly, Ma," he called.

"Well, there ain't been a purty Baxter since the name begun."

---

1. See kin you rout me out: Just see whether you can get me out of bed.
2. sacking: Made of reused cloth flour or sugar sacks.
3. eddied: Moved in a whirling motion, like a whirlpool or whirlwind.
4. breeches: Pants.

He wrinkled his nose at the mirror. The gesture made the freckles across the bridge blend together.

"I wisht I was dark like the Forresters."

"You be proud you ain't. Them fellers is black as their hearts.[5] You a Baxter and all the Baxters is fair."

"You talk like I wasn't no kin to you."

"My folks runs to fairness, too. They ain't none of 'em puny, though. Iffen you'll learn yourself to work, you'll be your Pa all over."

The mirror showed a small face with high cheek bones. The face was freckled and pale, but healthy, like a find sand. The hair grieved him on the occasions when he went to church or any doings at Volusia. It was straw-colored and shaggy, and no matter how carefully his father cut it, once a month on the Sunday morning nearest the full moon, it grew in tufts at the back. "Drakes' tails,"[6] his mother called them. His eyes were wide and blue. When he frowned, in close study over his reader, or watching something curious, they narrowed. It was then that his mother claimed him kin.

"He do favor[7] the Alverses a mite," she said.

Jody turned the mirror to inspect his ears; not for cleanliness, but remembering the pain of the day when Lem Forrester had held his chin with one vast hand and pulled his ears with the other.

"Boy, your ears is set up on your head like a 'possum's," Lem said.

Jody made a leering grimace at himself[8] and returned the mirror to the wall.

"Do we got to wait for Pa to eat breakfast?" he asked.

"We do. Set it all in front of you and there'd likely not be enough left for him."

He hesitated at the back door.

"And don't you slip off, neither. He ain't but to the corncrib."

From the south, beyond the black-jacks, he heard the bell-like voice of old Julia, giving tongue in great excitement. He thought he heard, too, his father, giving her a command. He bolted away before his mother's sharp voice could stop him. She, too, had heard the dog. She followed to the door and called after him.

"Don't you and your Pa be gone too long now, follerin' that fool hound. I'm o' no mind to set around waitin' breakfast and you two piddlin' around[9] in the woods."

He could no longer hear either old Julia or his father. He was in a frenzy for fear the excitement was over; the intruder gone

---

5. **black as their hearts:** Ma means that the Foresters are bad people.
6. **Drakes' tails:** So called because they look like a duck's tail.
7. **favor:** Resemble; look like.
8. **made a leering grimace at himself:** Made a face at himself in the mirror.
9. **piddlin' around:** Wasting time; goofing off.

and perhaps dog and father with it. He crashed through the black-jacks in the direction from which the sounds had come. His father's voice spoke, close at hand.

"Easy, son, What's done 'll wait for you."

He stopped short. Old Julia stood trembling, not in fear but in eagerness. His father stood looking down at the crushed and mangled carcass of black Betsy, the brood sow.[10]

"He must of heered me darin' him," Penny said. "Look careful, boy. See do you see what I see."

The sight of the mutilated[11] sow sickened him. His father was looking beyond the dead animal. Old Julia had her sharp nose turned in the same direction. Jody walked a few paces and examined the sand. The unmistakable tracks made his blood jump. They were the tracks of a giant bear. And from the print of the right front paw, as big as the crown of a hat, one toe was missing.

"Old Slewfoot!"

Penny nodded.

"I'm proud you remembered his track."

They bent together and studied the signs and the direction in which they had both come and gone.

"That's what I call," Penny said, "carryin' the war into the enemy's camp."

"None o' the dogs bayed him,[12] Pa. Lessen I didn't hear, for sleepin'."

"None of 'em bayed him. He had the wind in his favor. Don't you think he didn't know what he was doin'. He slipped in like a shadow and done his meanness and slipped out afore day."

A chill ran along Jody's backbone. He could picture the shadow, big and black as a shed in motion, moving among the black-jacks and gathering in the tame and sleeping sow with one sweep of the great clawed paw. Then the white tusks followed into the backbone, crushing it, and into the warm and palpitating[13] flesh. Betsy had had no chance even to squeal for help.

"He'd a 'ready fed," Penny pointed out. "He ate no more'n a mouthful. A bear's stomach is shrunk when he first comes outen his winter bed. That's why I hate a bear. A creetur that kills and eats what he needs, why, he's jest like the rest of us, makin' out the best he kin. But an animal, or a person either, that'll do harm jest to be a-doin'—You look in a bear's face and you'll see he's got no remorse."[14]

"You aim to carry in old Betsy?"

---

10. **brood sow:** Female pig kept for breeding.
11. **mutilated:** (myōōt′ lāt əd): Cut and torn.
12. **bayed him:** Howled upon scenting the bear.
13. **palpitating** (pal′ pə tāt ing): Quivering.
14. **remorse:** Regret; repentance.

"The meat's bad tore up, but I reckon there's sausage left. And lard."

Jody knew that he should feel badly about old Betsy, but all that he could feel was excitement. The unwarranted[15] kill, inside the sanctuary of the Baxter acres, had made a personal enemy of the big bear that had evaded all the stock owners for five years. He was wild to begin the hunt. He acknowledged to himself, as well, a trace of fear. Old Slewfoot had struck close to home.

He took one hind leg of the sow and Penny the other. They dragged it to the house with Julia reluctant at their heels. The old bear-dog could not understand why they did not set out at once on the chase.

"I'll swear," Penny said, "I'm daresome to break the news to your Ma."

"She'll rare for certain,"[16] Jody agreed.

"Betsy was sich a fine brood sow. My, she was fine."

Ma Baxter was waiting for them by the gate.

"I been a-callin' and I been a-callin'," she hailed them. "What you got there, piddlin' around so long? Oh dear goodness, oh dear goodness—my sow, my sow."

She threw her arms toward the sky. Penny and Jody passed through the gate and back of the house. She followed, wailing.

"We'll hang the meat to the cross-piece, son," Penny said. "The dogs'll not reach it there."

"You might tell me," Ma Baxter said. "The least you kin do is tell me, how come her dead and tore to ribbons right under my nose."

"Old Slewfoot done it, Ma," Jody said. "His tracks was certain."

"And them dogs asleep right here in the clearin'?"

The three had already appeared, nosing about the fresh smell of the blood. She threw a stick in their direction.

"You no-account creeturs![17] Hornin' in on our rations[18] and leavin' sich as this to happen."

"Ain't a dog borned as smart as that bear," Penny said.

"They could of barked."

She threw another stick and the dogs slunk away.

The family went to the house. In the confusion, Jody went first into the kitchen, where the smell of breakfast tortured him. His mother could not be too disturbed to notice what he was doing.

"You git right back here," she called, "and wash your dirty hands."

He joined his father at the water-shelf. Breakfast was on the table. Ma Baxter sat, swaying her body in distress, and did not

---

15. unwarranted: Unjustified; unprovoked.
16. She'll rare for certain: She'll surely be upset.
17. no-account creeturs: Worthless creatures.
18. Hornin' in on our rations: Eating our food.

eat. Jody heaped his plate. There were grits and gravy, hot cakes, and buttermilk.

"Anyway," he said, "we got meat to eat for a whiles now."

She turned on him.

"Meat now, and none this winter."

"I'll ask the Forresters out of a sow,"[19] Penny said.

"Yes, and be beholden to[20] them rascals." She began to wail again. "That blasted bear—I'd like to git my hands on him."

"I'll tell him when I see him," Penny said mildly between mouthfuls.

Jody burst out laughing.

"That's right," she said. "Make a fun-box outen me."

Jody patted her big arm.

"Hit jest come to me, Ma, how you'd look—you and ol' Slewfoot mixin' it."

"I'd bet on your Ma," Penny said.

"Nobody but me don't take life serious," she lamented.

---

19. **ask the Forresters out of a sow:** Ask the Forresters to give us a sow.
20. **be beholden to:** Owe a debt to.

☑ Check Your Comprehension

1. At what time of day does the story begin? What is Jody doing then?
2. Describe the situation that Jody discovers when he goes outside to find his Pa.
3. Why does Jody's father hate bears?
4. How does Jody feel about old Betsy's death?
5. Summarize Ma's reaction to old Betsy's death.

◆ Critical Thinking

INTERPRET

1. What kind of person is Ma? Support your answer with details from the story. **[Support]**

2. Compare Ma with Pa. How are they similar? How are they different? Use details from the story in your answer. **[Support]**

EVALUATE

3. What values do you think Ma and Pa are passing on to Jody, based on their behavior? **[Evaluate]**

APPLY

4. In what ways does Jody seem like a typical twelve-year-old boy that you might know? In what ways does he seem different? **[Compare and Contrast; Distinguish]**

Marjorie Kinnan Rawlings

Comparing and Connecting the Author's Works

◆ Literary Focus: Dialect

You may have noticed that people who come from the New England area may speak differently than people who come from the Midwestern or the Southern regions of the United States. Some residents of different regions speak a different dialect of English. **Dialects** are different forms of the same language spoken by people in a particular region or group. Dialects may differ from the standard form of a language in pronunciation, grammar, and word choice.

In her writing, Marjorie Kinnan Rawlings uses the Southern dialect of northern, rural Florida to bring her characters vividly and realistically to life. The use of dialect can help readers imagine a way of life that may be very different from their own.

Understanding Dialect

1. Rewrite these examples of dialect from "Antses in Tim's Breakfast" and the selection from *The Yearling,* using spelling, grammar, and vocabulary that reflect the way you usually speak.

   You and the hounds and all the rest of the stock. Mighty lovin' on an empty belly and me with a dish in my hand.

   They ain't no screens to the house and the skeeters like to eat us alive. And I cain't keep the antses outen Tim's breakfast.

2. In the story, turn back to the passages that you rewrote above. Are they as effective at portraying character when they are rewritten in standard English? Why or why not?

◆ Drawing Conclusions About the Author's Work

Marjorie Kinnan Rawlings loved her life in the rural backwoods of Florida, despite its hardships. She greatly admired the people of the area for their self-reliance and their closeness to nature. She once described them as "beautiful in their repose, their dignity, their self-respect." According to critic Gordon E. Bigelow, "Her concern to present this people and their way of life…as something beautiful was so strong that she felt she had failed as an artist when anyone read her books and was left with a sense of ugliness."

After reading the two selections, what impression do you have of the Florida backcountry, its people, and their way of life in the first half of the twentieth century? Use a herringbone organizer like the one below to organize your thoughts. Write the central idea—impressions of rural Florida—on the central line. Then use the lines on the diagonal spines to record passages from the selections that describe things or personal qualities you found beautiful or ugly. When your organizer is complete, write an essay that summarizes your impressions of the world presented in Rawlings' work.

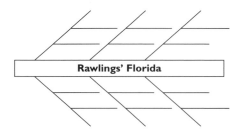

Rawlings' Florida

◆ Idea Bank

Writing

1. **Letter** Take the role of Marjorie Kinnan Rawlings. You are a newcomer to Cross Creek, and Tim's wife has just told you about the difficulties she faces every day. Write a letter to one of your friends in the city, describing the incident and how you feel about it.

2. **Dialogue in Dialect** Sit in a cafeteria, park, or mall, and listen to the people around you talk. Take notes on any distinctive grammar, pronunciation, slang, or other word choices that people use in their conversations. Then write a dialogue, using the dialect of your own region or group. Spell words the way you think people around you pronounce them.

3. **Advice Booklet** Write a guide for families moving from one kind of community—city, suburb, or rural area—to another. Point out that newcomers to any area can expect some differences in lifestyle, attitudes, and behavior. Provide advice on how to adapt to the changes. **[Social Studies Link]**

Speaking and Listening

4. **Dramatic Reading** With a partner, choose a passage of dialogue from one of the selections, and read it aloud for the class. As you rehearse your performance, make sure you understand the feelings each character is trying to express. **[Performing Arts Link]**

Researching and Representing

5. **Bulletin Board** Read *The Yearling* in its entirety, and watch the acclaimed 1946 film version starring Gregory Peck and Jane Wyman. Then design a bulletin board comparing your impressions of the work's characters and setting as presented in the two different media. **[Media Link]**

6. **Field Guide** Research the trees and other plants of northern Florida. Then select five plants and write an illustrated field guide to them, giving each plant's scientific name and classification, describing its life cycle and the climate in which it grows, and telling how to recognize it. **[Science Link; Art Link]**

◆ Further Reading, Listening, and Viewing

- Rawlings, Marjorie Kinnan: *Cross Creek* (1942). In this heartwarming memoir, Rawlings describes her struggles to survive in the backcountry, the unforgettable people she came to love, and her deep sense of connection to a harsh but beautiful land.

- *Cross Creek* (1983). Videocassette. This film version of Rawlings' memoir stars Mary Steenburgen and Rip Torn, and focuses on the true story that inspired the novel *The Yearling*.

- *The Yearling* (1946). Videocassette. The film version of this classic stars Gregory Peck, Jane Wyman, and a young actor named Claude Jarman, Jr., who won an Academy Award for his performance.

On the Web:

http://www.phschool.com/atschool/literature
Go to the student edition *Bronze*. Proceed to Unit 7. Then, click Hot Links to find Web sites featuring Marjorie Kinnan Rawlings.

Rod Serling In Depth

> "You unlock this door with the key of imagination. . . . you're moving into a land of both shadow and substance, of things and ideas. You've just crossed over into . . . the Twilight Zone."
>
> —*Rod Serling*

ROD SERLING was born in Syracuse, New York, on December 25, 1924, but spent most of his childhood in Binghamton, New York, a place that always lived on in his imagination. Rod was an outgoing, popular boy with a vivid imagination. He and his older brother loved to read the stories in popular fantasy magazines such as *Amazing Stories* and *Weird Tales.* If they saw a movie together, they would come home and act out all the parts together. Serling was a leader in high school. He acted in class plays and was the editor of his high school newspaper.

Harsh Realities On the day he graduated from high school in 1942, Serling enlisted in the United States Army as a paratrooper, a dangerous choice when the nation was in the middle of fighting World War II. After basic training, Serling was sent to the Philippines as part of an assault and demolitions team. He received a severe shrapnel wound in battle and was sent to the hospital. Bitter and restless when he returned home after the war, Serling said he turned to writing to express his feelings.

A Career in Broadcasting After the war, Serling attended Antioch College in Ohio, where he majored in literature and began writing original radio dramas for the college radio station. In 1949 he entered one of his scripts in a national contest and won second prize—a check for five hundred dollars and a trip to New York City.

Encouraged, Serling began submitting scripts to radio shows—and received forty rejections before making his first sale. After graduating from college in 1950, he took a job as a staff writer with a Cincinnati radio station, but found the job creatively unsatisfying. Serling continued to write dramatic scripts for radio on his own time.

Breaking into Television In 1951 Serling sold a script to the Lux Video Theatre series, which then quickly bought ten more of his scripts. By 1953, he was able to quit his job in Cincinnati and become a full-time freelance writer. Serling produced more than seventy scripts for television from 1951–1955.

Reaching the Big Time In 1955 Serling wrote a television drama called *Patterns,* a realistic look at ruthless corporate politics. The play was a big hit and was rebroadcast by popular demand, the first television drama to receive this honor. It also won Serling critical acclaim and his first Emmy Award. *Patterns* was followed by two-more Emmy winners, *Requiem for a Heavyweight* in 1956 and *The Comedian* in 1957. Suddenly, Rod Serling was a highly-regarded writer.

Battling the Censors and Entering the Twilight Zone Serling was a serious writer with a strong social conscience, and many of his scripts dealt with controversial social issues of the 1950's. Television, however, was ruled by networks and advertising sponsors, who wanted to avoid controversial programming.

Serling faced increasing battles over censorship of his work, especially with his dramas *A Town Has Turned to Dust* (about racial prejudice) and *The Rank and File* (about corruption in labor unions). Weary of fighting the censors, Serling turned to fantasy in 1959, and the now legendary *Twilight Zone* was born.

A Television Legend *The Twilight Zone* was broadcast from 1959–1964. The stories featured memorable characters, mysterious plots, and often disturbing themes. They raised intriguing questions about science and superstition, good and evil, innocence and guilt, success and failure, dreams and reality, and isolation and community.

Of 156 episodes, more than half were written by Serling himself. *The Twilight Zone* became a showcase for other writers too, including Ray Bradbury and Richard Matheson, as well as for up-and-coming actors such as Robert Redford, Burt Reynolds, and William Shatner.

Beyond the Twilight Zone After *The Twilight Zone,* Serling wrote or co-wrote scripts for movies such as *Seven Days in May* (1964) and *Planet of the Apes* (1968). He launched a new science-fiction series called *Night Gallery* in 1970, but it never attained either the critical or popular success of The *Twilight Zone.*

From 1968–1975 Serling taught writing seminars at Ithaca College and gave lectures at other colleges across the country. He died on June 28, 1975 following complications during surgery.

◆ The Golden Age of Television

Although television broadcasting began in the 1930's, only a few hundred people owned television sets, and there were very few programs. It wasn't until after World War II, when millions of soldiers came home and bought houses, that television ownership and television programming expanded.

The film industry in Hollywood felt threatened by the new medium and refused to release any of its stars or movies for television broadcast. As a result, the television industry, centered in New York City, was forced to develop its own original programming. Television recruited thousands of directors, writers, actors, and technicians from New York's theatres, and early television became, in effect, an "electronic Broadway," exposing millions of Americans to their first taste of live drama. Among the writers who created plays for television at this time were Rod Serling, Paddy Chayefsky, and Reginald Rose.

◆ Literary Works

Television Dramas
- *Patterns* (1955)
- *Requiem for a Heavyweight* (1956)
- *The Comedian* (1957)
- *The Twilight Zone* (1959–1964)

Movie Screenplays
- *The Yellow Canary* (1963)
- *Seven Days in May* (1964)
- *Assault on a Queen* (1966)
- *Planet of the Apes* (1968, co-written with Michael Wilson)
- *The Man* (1972)

Books
- *Patterns: Four Television Plays with the Author's Personal Commentary* (1957)
- *Stories from the Twilight Zone* (1960)
- *More Stories from the Twilight Zone* (1961)
- *Requiem for a Heavyweight* (1962)
- *Night Gallery* (1971)
- *Rod Serling's Other Worlds* (1978)

Rod Serling

from About Writing for Television

There is probably no single "absolute" anyone can use as a yardstick to describe the nature of the television writer, his background, his fortes,[1] or the nature of his advent[2] into the realm of television writing—save for the simple statement that there are no absolutes.

The TV writer is never trained to be a TV writer. There are no courses, however specialized and applied, that will catapult him into the profession. And it was especially true back in the twilight days of radio that coincided with the primitive beginnings of television that the television playwrights evolved[3]—and were never born. In my case the decision to become a television writer arose from no professional master plan. I was on the writing staff of a radio station in the Midwest. Staff writing is a particularly dreamless occupation characterized by assembly-line writing almost around the clock. It is a highly variable occupation— everything from commercials and fifteen-second public-service announcements to half-hour documentary dramas. In a writing sense, it serves its purpose. It teaches a writer discipline, a time sense for any kind of mass-media writing, and a technique. But it also dries up his creativity, frustrates him, and tires him out.

It's axiomatic[4] that the beginning free-lance writer must have some sort of economic base from which he operates. Usually it is a job with at least a subsistence[5] wage to give him rent money and three square meals a day while he begins the treacherous and highly unsure first months of writing on his own. The most desirable situation encompasses[6] an undemanding job that draws little out of the writer's mind during the working day so that his nocturnal writing will be fresh, inspired and undiverted. In my case this was a wish but never a reality.

I used to come home at seven o'clock in the evening, gulp down a dinner and set up my antique portable typewriter on the kitchen table. The first hour would then be spent closing all the mental gates and blacking out all the impressions of a previous eight hours of writing. You have to have a pretty selective brain for this sort of operation. There has to be the innate ability to single-track the creative processes. And after a year or so of this

---

1. **fortes** (fortz or for´ tāz): Strengths; strong points; things a person does well.
2. **advent** (ad´ vent): Arrival; entry.
3. **evolved** (ē välvd´): Developed gradually.
4. **axiomatic** (ak´ sē ə mat´ ik): Self-evident; well-established.
5. **subsistence** (səb sis´ təns): Enough to survive on.
6. **encompasses** (en kum´ pəs əz): Includes.

kind of problem, you have rent receipts, fuel for the furnace and a record of regular eating; but you have also denied yourself, as I did, a basic "must" for every writer. And this is simple solitude—physical and mental.

The process of writing cannot be juggled with another occupation. The job of creating cannot be compartmentalized[7] with certain hours devoted to one kind of creation and other hours set aside for still another. Writing is a demanding profession and a selfish one. And because it is selfish and demanding, because it is compulsive and exacting, I didn't embrace it. I succumbed[8] to it.

---

7. compartmentalized (käm´ pärt ment´ l īzd): Set aside in a separate compartment or area.
8. succumbed (sə kumd´): Gave in; yielded.

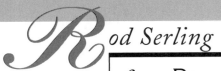
Rod Serling

from Requiem for a Heavyweight

Harlan McClintock is a has-been prizefighter, too old to fight and uncertain of what to do next.

ACT TWO

We dissolve to an anteroom of a small office with a sign on the door: "New York State Employment Office." Sitting on a bench are McClintock and Army. McClintock appears nervous and fidgety. He is constantly running a finger through his collar, which is much too tight, as is his suit, shirt and everything else he wears. He looks helplessly at Army, who pats his arm reassuringly.

ARMY.
You look fine. Don't worry. You look just great.

MCCLINTOCK.
(In a whisper): But what do I say, Army?

ARMY.
What d'ya mean, what d'ya say? Just tell her you want a job, that's all. It's simple.

MCCLINTOCK.
But what kind of a job?

ARMY.
You don't have to worry about that. You just tell her the sort of thing you can do and it's up to them to find you one.

MCCLINTOCK.
Army, in the past two days I've been thirty-five places already. Most of these jokers won't even let me in the door.

ARMY.
It's different here. This place is official. They're here just to get people jobs. People like you that can't find them easy on their own.
At this moment a young woman appears at the door of the inner office.

GRACE.
Mr. McClintock, please.
> *McClintock bolts to his feet, almost upsetting Army.*

MCCLINTOCK.
That's me! That's me!

GRACE.
(Smiling): In here, please, Mr. McClintock.
> *McClintock turns to Army and grabs his arm.*

ARMY.
(Firmly removing his fingers): I'm right here at ringside, but I can't go in to fight for you. Go ahead.
> *McClintock, with another journey of his finger through his collar, walks hesitantly after the young woman. We pan[1] with them into her office as the door closes. He turns around with a start at its closing.*

GRACE.
Sit down, Mr. McClintock. Right over here, please, near the desk.

MCCLINTOCK.
Thanks. Thank you very much.
> *He sits down with another eye toward the door.*
> *They both start to speak together.*

MCCLINTOCK.
I was—

GRACE.
Now, Mr. McClintock—

MCCLINTOCK.
I was just wondering if . . . Oh, I beg your pardon.

GRACE.
You were going to say?

MCCLINTOCK.
I was just wondering if my friend could come in?

---

1. pan: Camera movement that enables viewers to take in a large scene or to follow a character's movements.

GRACE.
Is he looking for employment too?

MCCLINTOCK.
No. No, not exactly, but . . . well, he's kind of my handler.[2]

GRACE.
I beg your pardon?

MCCLINTOCK.
(Wets his lips): It's okay. He'll stay out there.
>   *She looks at him and smiles, then glances at a sheet of paper.*

GRACE.
Harlan McClintock. Your age is—

MCCLINTOCK.
Thirty-three.
>   *She makes a little notation with a pencil.*

GRACE.
Place of birth?

MCCLINTOCK.
Kenesaw, Tennessee.

GRACE.
I see. Your education? *(She looks up at him)* Mr. McClintock, you left that blank here.

MCCLINTOCK.
My education? You mean school?

GRACE.
That's right.

MCCLINTOCK.
Ninth grade.

GRACE.
Then you left, is that it?

---

2. **handler:** Person who trains or manages a boxer.

MCCLINTOCK.
(Nodding): Then I left.

GRACE.
Now, field of interest.

MCCLINTOCK.
I beg your pardon?

GRACE.
Your field of interest. What do you like to do?

MCCLINTOCK.
Most anything. I don't much care.

GRACE.
(Looks down at his sheet and frowns slightly): Past employment record, Mr. McClintock. You have nothing written down there. *(She looks up at him)* Who've been your past employers?

MCCLINTOCK.
Well . . . you see . . . I really haven't had past employ-ers—I mean, past employers like you mean down on that sheet. I've always been kind of on my own, except you might say I've been working for Maish.

GRACE.
Maish?

MCCLINTOCK.
You see, all I've been doing the past fourteen years is fightin'.

GRACE.
Fighting.

MCCLINTOCK.
That's right. You know, in the ring.

GRACE.
You mean a prize fighter?

MCCLINTOCK.
(Smiles): That's right. Prize fighter.

GRACE.

A professional prize fighter.

MCCLINTOCK.

(Delightedly): Yeah, that's it. You catch on. A professional prize fighter. Heavyweight.

> *Grace stares at him for a moment and we cut to a tight close-up of McClintock's face as he becomes conscious of her stare. He almost unconsciously puts one hand across his face to hide the scar tissue. He turns his face away ever so slightly. Grace notices this and turns away herself, and then looks down again at the paper.*

GRACE.

That sounds like interesting work, Mr. McClintock.

MCCLINTOCK.

(Looking up at her): Well, it's . . . it's a living. I don't want you to go to no trouble. Army says I should just tell you that . . . well, anything you got's jake[3] with me. Dishwashing—anything.

> *She looks at him again for a long moment.*

GRACE.

(Kindly): Let's see if we can't examine something else, Mr. McClintock—something you might like even more. How about factory work?

MCCLINTOCK.

(Shaking his head): I never worked in a factory. I wouldn't know anything about it.

GRACE.

No sort of assembly-line work, blueprint reading, anything like that? *(He shakes his head, she wets her lips)* Anything in sales, Mr. McClintock? There's a lot of openings in that sort of thing now. Department-store work. Anything like that?

MCCLINTOCK.

(Shaking his head): I . . . I couldn't do anything like that. I couldn't sell nothin'. *(Then with a kind of lopsided grin)* With my face I'd scare away the customers.

---

3. **jake:** Okay.

He laughs lightly at this and when he looks up she is staring at him, not laughing with him at all. He becomes embarrassed now and half rises to his feet.

MCCLINTOCK.
Look, Miss, I don't want to take up your time. *(And now in his hopelessness the words come out; he forgets his embarrassment)* The only reason I come is because Army said I should come. I've been answering all these ads like I told ya and I've been getting no place at all. Maish needs the dough real bad and I can't do nothin' for him any more, and I got to. I got to get some kind of a job. Don't make any difference what I do. Anything at all.

GRACE.
Mr. McClintock—

MCCLINTOCK.
(Unaware of her now): A guy goes along fourteen years. All he does is fight. Once a week, twice a week, prelims,[4] semifinals, finals. He don't know nothin' but that. All he can do is fight. Then they tell him no more. And what's he do? What's he supposed to do? What's he supposed to know how to do besides fight? They got poor Maish tied up by the ears and I got to do somethin' for him. *(He looks down at his hands. He pauses for a moment)*

GRACE.
(Quietly): Mr. McClintock, we handle a lot of placements here. I'm sure we can find you something—

MCCLINTOCK.
I know you're going to do the best you can, but . . .
(He points to the paper on her desk) I don't fit in any of the holes. I mean that question there. Why did you leave your last job? State reason.

GRACE.
That's question nine. You see, Mr. McClintock—

---

4. prelims: Preliminaries, the less important boxing matches that precede the main event.

MCCLINTOCK.

I understand it but what do I write down? What do I write down that would make sense? I left my last job because I got hit so much that I was on my way to punchy land and I'd probably go blind. How would that read there?

GRACE.

(Her eyes narrow): Punchy land?

MCCLINTOCK.

Sure. You fight so long and then you walk around on your heels listening to the bells. That's what happens to you. Doc looks at my eyes, says one or two more I might go blind.

GRACE.

(Very softly): I see.

MCCLINTOCK.

(Getting excited again): And that's not fair. It's a dirty break, that's all. In 1948 they ranked me number five. I'm not kidding ya. Number five. And that wasn't any easy year neither. There was Charles and Wolcott and Louis[5] still around. And they had me up there at number five. Maish was sure that—

GRACE.

Maish? Who's Maish, Mr. McClintock?

MCCLINTOCK.

Maish is my manager. And where does it leave him? That's a nice thing to do to a guy who's kept you going for fourteen years. You stop cold on him. So it's a bum break. It ain't fair at all. *(He rises and turns his back to her, and he slowly subsides[6])* I'm . . . I'm real sorry, Miss. I didn't mean to blow up like that. You ought to kick me out of here. Honest, I'm real sorry.

---

5. Charles and Wolcott and Louis: Mack Charles, Jersey Joe Walcott, and Joe Louis were all heavyweight boxers during the 1940's. Joe Louis was heavyweight champion from 1937-1949. Mack Charles was champion from 1950-1951, and Jersey Joe Walcott became heavyweight champion in 1951.

6. subsides (səb sīdz´): Dies down; becomes less intense.

GRACE.

(Again quietly): That's perfectly all right, Mr. McClintock.
As long as you've got your address down here we'll contact you if anything comes up, and we'll—

> *She stops, staring across the room at him—at the*
> *big shoulders that are slumped in front of her and*
> *the big hands down by his sides that clench and*
> *unclench. A certain softness shows in her face—*
> *a pitying look. She wets her lips and then forces*
> *a smile.*

GRACE.

Right after the war I did a lot of work with disabled vet-
erans.

> *As soon as she has said this she is sorry. His head*
> *jerks up and he turns slowly toward her.*

MCCLINTOCK.

Yeah? Go on.

GRACE.

I meant . . . I meant you'd be surprised the . . . the
different kinds of openings that come up for— *(She*
struggles for a word)

MCCLINTOCK.

For cripples. For those kind of guys?

GRACE.

I didn't mean just that. I meant for people who have special problems.

MCCLINTOCK.

I've got no special problems. *(He takes a step toward her)*
There wasn't no place on that question sheet of yours—
but I was almost the heavyweight champion of the world.
I'm a big ugly slob and I look like a freak, but I was
almost the heavyweight champion of the world. I'd like to
put that down some place on that paper. This isn't just a
punk. This was a guy who was almost the heavyweight
champion of the world!

He slams his fist on the desk, and then as quickly as the anger came it leaves. Very slowly he takes his hand from the desk. He looks at it briefly, closes his eyes and turns away again. He looks down at his hand and feels of the bruise over his eye. He looks away from her. Grace is staring at him all the time.

GRACE.
Did you hurt your hand, Mr. McClintock?

MCCLINTOCK.
(Looks at his hand): I guess I did. That's the . . . that's the thing of it. When you go for so long the hurt piles up and you don't even feel them. You get out of the ring and you go back to a dressing room and you look in the mirror. You look like somebody just ran over you with a tractor—but somehow it doesn't seem to hurt. There's always a reason for it. You know that . . . you know that you just took another step up. Then after the last one—when the wad's all shot[7] and you're over the hill and there aren't going to be any more—then suddenly you do start to hurt. The punches you got fourteen years ago—even then. And when Maish and the Doc and Army—they were all standing around me that night and I heard somebody say, He's wound up.[8] Then it hurts. Then it hurts like you've got to scream. Like now. It hurts now. Before, at least—before every little piece of skin they took off you—was part of the bill you had to pay. And then all of a sudden one night you have to throw all the fourteen years out into an alley and you know then that you've been paying that bill for nothing.
We cut to a very tight close-up of Grace's face as she comes around from behind her desk. She touches his arm tentatively.

GRACE.
Mr. McClintock, I think . . . I think we can get you something you'll like. Just give us time.

MCCLINTOCK.
(Looks at her): Something I'll like? Do that, Miss. I don't want much. Just . . . the heavyweight championship of the world. That's all.

---

7. **when the wad's all shot:** When your luck runs out.
8. **wound up:** Finished; washed up.

He stares at her and you can see in his face that he wants to say something—wants to apologize, wants to explain to her that this is a bitterness directed at no one, but it can't come out, it can't be articulated.⁹ He turns slowly and walks out of the room. She stands there watching him through the open door. We see Army rise. The two men exchange words and then they both leave. Grace slowly closes the door, goes back to her desk pensively.¹⁰ We take a slow fade-out on her face.

---

9. **articulated** (ar tik´ yə lāt əd): Put into words; expressed.
10. **pensively** (pen´ siv lē): As in deep thought; in a sad, serious way.

☑ Check Your Comprehension

1. What does Serling say he learned from his staff writing job in radio?
2. What unfortunate effects did the staff writing job have on Serling?
3. According to Serling, why can't serious writing be juggled with another occupation?
4. In "Requiem for a Heavyweight," what problems does McClintock face when he goes to the employment office?
5. At the end of the scene from "Requiem for a Heavyweight," why is McClintock angry?

◆ Critical Thinking

INTERPRET

1. In "About Writing for Television," what does Serling mean when he says that he didn't "embrace" the writing profession but "succumbed" to it? **[Interpret]**
2. In "Requiem for a Heavyweight," why does McClintock express such a wide range of feelings about his career—from embarrassment to pride to bitterness? **[Connect]**
3. The word *requiem* refers to music or religious services for the dead. Why might Serling have chosen to call his television play, "Requiem for a Heavyweight"? **[Interpret]**

EXTEND

4. Today, it is quite common to pursue several careers in the course of a lifetime. Brainstorm with classmates for a list of possible careers that McClintock might enjoy. **[Career Link]**

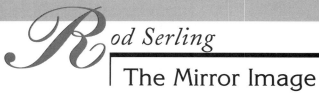

The Mirror Image

The cold November rain was beating at the big front windows of the City Bus Terminal, blurring the dim lights along the street and the driveway. It was as if grim, black night had gathered the building in its all-enveloping[1] folds, turning the terminal into a small, detached world of its own.

On a night as bad for travel as this, the place was almost deserted. Ticket office, baggage room, lunch counter, all were staying open only because they usually did, until the last bus arrived. Tonight, however, prospective[2] passengers were very few. There was an elderly couple seated on a wooden bench at one end of the terminal; and a girl in her early twenties at the other.

The girl's name was Millicent Barnes, and she was fidgety enough to make up for a whole busload of passengers. She kept looking at her wrist watch and comparing it with the big clock over the door. She looked at the ticket window, where a complacent[3] ticket agent was reading a magazine; then at the baggage room, which was deserted, and finally to the lunch counter, where a patient, middle-aged woman was putting things in order for the next day.

Millicent's own patience must have reached its limit, for suddenly she arose, walked over to the ticket window and rapped its grating to rouse the agent's attention. As he looked up, Millicent asked crisply:

"The bus to Cortland. It was due half an hour ago. When will it be in?"

"She'll be in when she'll be in." The agent laid his magazine aside and gave the girl a fixed stare. "I told you that the last time you asked, and the time before."

"Why, the only times I've asked is right now!" exclaimed Millicent. "All I want is a civil answer from you—"

She broke off abruptly, staring into the baggage room, which connected with the ticket office. There by itself, was a bright blue suitcase, with brass trim, somewhat the worse for wear, as indicated by its taped handle. Millicent swung about, stared back at the bench that she had just left. There was her own bag, identical in every detail, even to the taped handle and a red baggage stub attached to it.

---

1. **all-enveloping** (en vel′ əp ing): Completely wrapping or covering; completely surrounding.
2. **prospective** (prə spek′ tiv): Expected in the future; likely to become.
3. **complacent** (kəm plā sənt): Self-satisfied; pleased with oneself.

Millicent started toward the bench, then pressed her hand to her eyes, turned around and went back to the ticket window, where the agent said caustically:[4]

"Well? Shall we run through it all again?"

"I want to know more about that suitcase," returned Millicent. "The one in the baggage room. It looks just like mine."

"And why shouldn't it? It is yours. You checked it just a little while ago."

"But it can't be my bag. That's mine, over there—"

Millicent turned, gesturing to the bench, only to break off again. There was no bag there!

Now the ticket agent was mingling sarcasm with a bit of sympathy:

"Why don't you go over there and sit down, miss? You're walking in your sleep, or you're seeing things, or something. Just rest quiet and let me read my magazine. When the Cortland bus comes in, you'll hear a big roar from the motor, and you'll see people walk in through that door. Then you'll know the bus is ready."

"But I—I can't remember check my bag—"

Somewhat dazed, Millicent walked past the bench and went over to the lunch counter, where she sat down and stared vacantly, until the counter woman asked, "Are you all right, miss?"

"Why, yes." Millicent studied her reflection in a mirror behind the counter. "Don't I look well?"

"You look fine, honey," the woman replied. "But you sat down and stared the same way when you came over here before."

"Why, I wasn't here before!" Millicent exclaimed. "What is this? I checked my bag without knowing it, I'm told I asked questions before about the bus. Now, you tell me—"

Millicent's thoughts broke off in the light of stern reality. While staring in the mirror, she had let her gaze revert to the reflection of the bench, to make sure that her suitcase hadn't returned there. It hadn't, but she had!

There, seated where she had been a short time before, Millicent saw the mirrored image of a girl who was her identical twin. Either that, or Millicent had become someone else and was looking back at her old self of ten minutes before.

"What can I get you, honey?" The counter woman's voice was worried. "A glass of water—a cup of coffee—maybe a cold cloth— or an aspirin?"

Millicent shook her head as she clutched the counter to keep from falling off the stool. From that angle, she could only see her

---

4. **caustically** (kôs′ tik lē): Sarcastically; critically.

own face in the mirror, and it was very white. But the coldness of the counter revived her enough to wrench herself full about and stare at the actual bench.

Her double was gone, but the suitcase was there!

Unsteadily, Millicent walked to the bench, keeping her eyes on the suitcase all the way. As she sat down, she pressed her hand on the bag, to make sure it was really there. She gave a challenging look at the ticket window, and the agent looked up from his magazine to return a knowing smile. Millicent arose, took a few compulsive steps toward the window, then decided to avoid another argument there.

If the ticket agent had seen Millicent's double, he might try to confuse her more. What Millicent wanted now were some witnesses in her own behalf, so she turned her steps to the other end of the waiting room and approached the elderly couple seated there. The man was dozing, but the woman was awake.

"I was wondering," said Millicent, "if you saw someone sitting in my seat, only a few minutes ago."

"Why, I don't think so, miss," the woman replied. "Of course, I wasn't particularly looking in that direction."

The elderly man heard the voices and awoke with a sudden start. Querulously,[5] he asked, "Has something happened? Is there any trouble?"

"No trouble." Millicent smoothed the situation hurriedly. "I thought I saw someone I knew. I'm sorry I disturbed you."

She went back past the ticket window, noting her own suitcase still by the bench. She was ready to have it out with the ticket agent, but first she threw a sharp glance at the baggage room, only to stop short with a double-take.

The room was empty, with no sign of the duplicate suitcase!

"What's happening to me?" Millicent breathed. "Am I having delusions?[6] Am I running a temperature?" She pressed her hand to her forehead. "No, I'm not even warm. No fever."

Millicent stiffened, realizing that her present actions were making her more conspicuous[7] and perhaps creating new suspicions in the minds of her watchers. She looked toward the door, tempted to rush out into the rain, if only to get a moment of relief from this growing feeling of madness. Right then, the door opened, and a tall man entered, shaking the rain from his hat brim and bringing an attaché case from the folds of his drenched topcoat.

---

5. **querulously** (kwer´ yōō ləs lē): Complainingly.
6. **delusions** (di lōō´ zhənz): False beliefs maintained in spite of all evidence to the contrary.
7. **conspicuous** (kən spik´ yū əs): Easily seen; clearly visible; standing out.

As he walked forward, the man pushed back his hat to reveal a smiling, friendly face. He was about thirty years of age, and apparently had traveled extensively, for he appraised the bus terminal in one sweeping glance. He was starting toward the ticket window, to make an inquiry there, when he suddenly turned toward Millicent, who was already coming to her feet.

"Your handbag," the man said politely, stooping to pick it up. "You just dropped it."

Numbly, Millicent realized that dropping a bag containing all her money was worse than forgetting what she had done with a suitcase. But she managed to return the man's smile as she murmured her thanks, so he asked her for information.

"The bus is late—I hope?"

"Yes, over a half an hour late. You mean the Cortland bus, don't you?"

"That's the one. If it wasn't late, I would have missed it for sure. I shouldn't even be here—"

The young man paused, noting how Millicent's smile had faded, showing her face to be drawn and white.

"Pardon me, miss." The man's tone showed concern. "You aren't ill, are you? Is there something I can do?"

"It's just that odd things have been happening. I've been—well, I guess I've been seeing things."

"Seeing things?" The man's smile broadened. "What sort of things?"

"Maybe I shouldn't tell you." Millicent gave a nervous laugh that seemed discordant[8] to her own ears. "You might call the police or an ambulance or something."

"Tell me, and maybe I can help. My name is Grinstead. Paul Grinstead. I'm from Binghamton."

"I'm Millicent Barnes." Her tone still hollow, she looked around almost wildly. "At least I *was* Millicent Barnes. I'm a private secretary, and I've just taken a new job in Buffalo. That's where I'm going tonight. To Buffalo."

Millicent finished on an earnest note, as though hoping to convince this new listener that she was sound of mind as well as sincere. Paul promptly responded in a similar vein.

"I was supposed to be in Syracuse tonight, but the planes are all grounded. I took a cab from Binghamton, and we got stuck in a ditch, and I had to hike two miles to get here." He took off his soaked overcoat, shook it, and draped it over the bench. "I'm about four hours away from Binghamton and about five minutes away from pneumonia." He paused to deliver his friendly smile. "That's my story; now go on with yours."

---

8. **discordant** (dis kôrd′ ənt): Not in agreement; not in harmony; clashing.

"It's not quite that rough," Millicent began. Then, with a sudden frown, she amended,[9] "Maybe it's rougher. All my trouble has been right here in this bus station. The ticket man says I've asked him about the bus three or four times, but I'm sure I only went to his window once. The woman at the lunch counter claims I was there before, but I'm sure I wasn't. And then, when I looked for my suitcase—"

Millicent broke off as she looked toward the end of the bench, then added with a suppressed[10] scream, "It's gone again!"

With a smile, Paul reached beyond his draped coat and brought the suitcase into sight, saying, "Sorry. I didn't mean to hide it."

"I thought for a moment it was starting all over again," Millicent confessed. "The ticket agent said I checked my suitcase, and there was one that looked just like it in the baggage room. But when I came back from the lunch counter, my bag was here, and the one in the baggage room was gone."

Paul glanced toward the ticket window and studied the drab-mannered man behind it. With a shrug, he remarked, "That character doesn't look energetic enough to go playing tricks with suitcases. Who else could be doing it?"

"No one," replied Millicent. "No one, unless"—she paused warily—"you'll listen if I go on, won't you?"

Paul Grinstead nodded. "Go on."

"When I looked in that mirror behind the lunch counter"—Millicent gestured in that direction—"I could see this bench where we are now, and I saw—I saw—"

"Just what did you see, Miss Barnes?"

"I saw *myself,* sitting on this very bench!"

In one brief moment, Millicent realized that she had raised the real issue too soon. With all his sympathy and understanding, Paul Grinstead couldn't quite accept that. Who could? Not even Millicent herself. With that, she decided to backtrack.

"You're thinking I had some kind of delusion," she declared frankly. "But I'm not really ill. I don't have a headache, I'm not running a fever. But it isn't just seeing things that don't exist. Why did the ticket man—why did the lunch counter woman— why did they both think they had seen me come there before?"

"I don't know," Paul replied. "It's tough to figure."

"It is tough," Millicent returned, confident that she was winning her point. "Because whoever it was—whatever it was, I saw the same thing. We all saw the same mirror image, which is about the best thing to call it. Maybe they're a couple of kooks"— Millicent's sweeping gesture included the ticket office and the

---

9. **amended** (ə mend´ əd): Made a change in; improved; corrected.
10. **suppressed** (sə prest´): Kept in; held back.

lunch counter, with their present personnel—"but I'm not. Maybe they see crazy things regularly—I might, too, if I spent my life behind a ticket window or a lunch counter, but—but—"

"But they shouldn't unload those ideas on you," Paul said. "Is that it?" Then, as Millicent nodded, he questioned, "You've never had any mental problems, have you?" He waited for her head-shake, then assured her, "Of course you haven't. That means there is an explanation somewhere."

"Right," Millicent agreed, "but like what?"

"Like somebody who looks like you—like somebody you know—maybe playing a joke on you—or something—"

Millicent's dander was really up by now.

"Look, Mr. Grinstead," she said firmly. "I know I'm shuffling off to Buffalo, and you're wading in from Binghamton or staggering on to Syracuse, whatever the case may be. What would you think if your double showed up here? Do you have any friends who would come this far for a gag?"

"I guess not." Paul spoke as though he had been fully con-vinced. "Why, they couldn't even get here to begin with."

"That's how I feel," agreed Millicent. "Maybe my problem was just frustration. From the moment I walked in here. I wanted to hear them call, 'All aboard the bus for Buffalo!' and my worries would have ended there. Wouldn't yours?"

"You're right, Millicent. The sooner we go somewhere—"

A great roar interrupted, punctuated by stabs of a bus horn that was followed by the throbbing whimper of a diesel motor. The ticket agent laid his magazine aside and bawled out the announcement:

"Bus now arriving for Cortland—Syracuse—Buffalo—"

Paul Grinstead picked up Millicent's suitcase and said, "Let's go." He had his coat over his other arm, and he was carrying his attaché case too, but his broad smile showed that he didn't mind. The elderly couple arose from the far bench and also moved toward the bus platform. With a genuine laugh, Millicent confided to Paul:

"That ticket agent really does see things. He said a crowd would be coming from the bus. But there's nobody getting off."

"Right," Paul acknowledged, "but we're getting on."

The elderly couple were first. The bus driver punched their tickets, handed back the stubs, then looked up, startled, at Millicent Barnes, whose face had gone dead white as she tried and failed to stifle a scream.

There, framed in the bus window, was a lone passenger, who either had arrived on the bus and stayed there or had slipped aboard unseen, ahead of everyone else, from this very bus sta-tion. That passenger's face was one that Millicent knew too well.

It was her own!

Now, Millicent was backing away toward the swinging door leading into the bus station. Then, with the same mad impulse that she had resisted earlier, she turned about and made a dash for freedom, but not out into the open. She was going back into the very trap that she had been so eager to escape, and Paul was hurrying after her.

He overtook her by the bench where they had met. He folded his coat inside out and bunched it as a pillow. The woman from the lunch counter brought the damp cloth that she had recommended earlier. Millicent was lying there, eyes closed, moaning slightly as the bus driver arrived and spoke to Paul.

"We've got to be on our way. Very late now. Are you and the lady coming, or aren't you?"

Paul Grinstead shook his head.

"We'll wait for the next bus."

The ticket agent shambled over from the booth to put in his say:

"Next one ain't due until seven in the morning. You've got a long wait."

"We waited long enough for this one," returned Paul, "and we don't have to be anywhere until tomorrow, anyway."

The bus driver turned and went out to the platform, calling, "Okay, folks! We're on our way!" a mingling of roar and rumble followed, and the bus was off.

Silence resumed its sway at the City Bus Terminal, but it was a deeper silence than before. The ticket agent flicked off some of the lights, reciting, "When not in use, turn off the juice. That's my motto." In the gloom that followed, the lunch counter woman came over and spoke to Paul.

"I'm closing for the night and going home. I hope she gets to feel better." The woman gestured toward Millicent, who by now appeared to be asleep. "But, offhand, I'd say she needs medical help"—the woman tapped her forehead as she spoke—"if you know what I mean."

The counter woman practically had to feel her way out of the bus terminal, for it was almost dark now. Anyone coming in would be guided by a few dim lights, and the ticket booth, where the agent had resumed his reading, served as a final beacon. In fact, it was the light from that caged window that vaguely illuminated the bench where Millicent was lying, throwing a pattern of darkened cross-lines upon the girl's huddled form, while Paul watched from the shadows beyond.

For seemingly interminable minutes that tableau[11] continued. It might have lasted until passengers began arriving for the early

---

11. **tableau** (tab lō´): Striking scene made up of silent, motionless participants.

morning bus—as they would be doing, four or five hours from now—but suddenly Millicent stirred. She looked up, as though wondering whether to be soothed or frightened by the surrounding gloom. As she saw Paul's face leaning toward her in the crisscrossed light, she gave a smile of half-recognition.

"The bus?" she queried. "You didn't take it?"

"No," replied Paul. "I stayed to look after you. There will be another bus in a few hours. You're feeling better now?"

"A lot better." Millicent was staring up at the ceiling. "I once read something about parallel planes of existence, like twin worlds side by side. Each of us has a counterpart in the other plane, and sometimes the two worlds converge. The counterpart steps into our place and takes over. Maybe—maybe the woman I saw—maybe she was my counterpart—"

"Snap out of it, Millicent!" Paul interrupted. "There's got to be a more rational explanation. Anyway, we won't have to wait for that bus. I have a friend in Tully. I'll call him and have him bring his car down here and drive us to Syracuse. All right?"

Millicent nodded, then closed her eyes again. Paul walked over to the ticket window and asked for change to make a phone call. The ticket agent had heard all that was said, and now he expressed his opinions with a snort:

"Parallel planes! Twin worlds! No wonder she's off her rocker, believing that stuff. Are you going to call your friend in Tully? The one with the car?"

"I haven't any friend in Tully," Paul confided. "I just wanted to make it easier for her. She needs medical help, so I guess I'd better call the police. What do you think?"

"A good idea. She gives me the willies,[12] and I'd just as soon she got out of here, somehow."

While Paul was making his phone call, Millicent arose unsteadily and approached the lunch counter, where she sat on a stool and studied her reflected image in the mirror.

"Are you somebody else?" she whispered. "If you are, then tell me—who am I?"

Approaching footsteps brought her about, startled; but she smiled wanly when she saw it was Paul. Casually, he suggested: "Let's take a walk out by the bus platform. The rain is letting up, and the fresh air will do us good."

As they reached the platform, Millicent halted at sight of a police car. She gasped, threw an accusing look at Paul and tried to run, too late. Two officers grabbed her and pushed her into the rear seat. One got in with her, the other took the wheel and the police car pulled away. Glumly, Paul returned to the waiting

---

12. **She gives me the willies:** She makes me nervous; she gives me the creeps.

room, picked up Millicent's suitcase and took it to the ticket window, where he told the ticket agent:

"I got her off all right. They're taking her to the hospital for observation. They'll pick up her suitcase later."

"I'll put it in the baggage room."

"By the way," added Paul, "awhile ago, she told me that you insisted she had already checked her suitcase."

"She said I said that?" The ticket agent shook his head, amazed. "Boy! She wasn't only seeing things—she was hearing things, too!" He gestured to the bench. "Better get yourself a snooze, mister. You've got four and a half hours to wait."

Paul laid his attaché case on the end of the bench and tried it as a pillow, but it was too uncomfortable. He became restless and began to walk about, as Millicent had. He reached the lunch counter, sat down on the same stool and stared in the mirror. His gaze took in the bench, and his eyes went wide and startled.

His attaché case was gone!

Excitedly, Paul Grinstead rushed to the ticket window and began to rattle the bars. The ticket agent looked up from his magazine, as Paul gestured toward the bench, exclaiming:

"My attaché case—it's gone! Who took it?"

"Who took it?" the agent echoed. "There's nobody here but you and me, mister, and I haven't been away from this window."

Paul's sweeping glance took in the doorway to the bus platform, and he was sure he saw a figure in its shadows. He raced there, shouting, "There he is!" only to halt abruptly.

Facing him, as though reflected in a mirror, Paul saw a human figure, the exact counterpart of himself. Then, as he blinked, that living image was gone. Madly, Paul dashed out to the platform, shouting, "Hey, there! Wait!"

Paul Grinstead found himself alone. He was staring one way, then the other, his hair disheveled, his face streaked with sweat, his eyes stricken with fear. He shouted louder:

"Who are you? Where are you? What are you doing here?"

Those repeated shouts reached the ticket agent, and he spoke into the telephone:

"Police? This is the bus terminal. Better get over and pick up the guy who called you about the girl. He's gone even battier than she did."

As he laid the phone down, the ticket agent added:

"Parallel planes! Twin worlds! Humph!"

Significant words for all persons planning an extended tour through the Twilight Zone. But don't expect to get your information from the window in your local bus terminal!

☑ Check Your Comprehension

1. In the bus terminal, what things does Millicent see that she can't explain?
2. Why is Millicent tempted to run out of the bus terminal and into the rain?
3. What does Millicent see as she is stepping onto the bus?
4. What theory about the mysterious events does Millicent offer to Paul Grinstead?
5. What trick does Paul play on Millicent?
6. Summarize what happens to Paul after Millicent leaves.

◆ Critical Thinking

INTERPRET

1. Do you think Paul's behavior towards Millicent has anything to do with what happens at the end of the story? [**Make a Judgement**]
2. One critic has said that many *Twilight Zone* episodes express the following cautionary message: "Man can never be too sure of anything." Explain how the story "Mirror Image" conveys that message. [**Support**]

APPLY

3. Could Millicent or Paul have done something differently that might have changed the outcome of the story? What consequences might have followed from their change in behavior? [**Modify**]
4. At the end of the story, Paul is left alone with a mystery he can't explain. What do you think he should do next? [**Speculate**]

Rod Serling
Comparing and Connecting the Author's Works

◆ Literary Focus: Dialogue

Dialogue in a play, movie, or television drama is the words spoken by the actors. In drama, characters are developed entirely through their dialogue and actions. Usually, there is no narrator to tell us what the characters are thinking.

Good dialogue is realistic and easy to follow. It makes the audience feel that the people and situations they are watching are real. It also helps develop the plot conflicts. Critic Jeffrey Armstrong has said of Rod Serling that "perhaps his greatest strength as a writer was his handling of dialogue—always forceful and direct, with effective use of pauses and unusual wordplay."

1. Reread the opening pages of "Requiem for a Heavyweight."
   a) Does McClinctock's dialogue sound believably like that of an uneducated prize fighter? Why or why not?
   b) How does Serling use the dialogue to convey that McClintock is very nervous about the job interview?
2. Reread the scene in "The Mirror Image" in which Millicent meets Paul.
   a) Does the dialogue realistically convey how two strangers might speak to each other in this situation? Why or why not? b) Does Paul's dialogue convince you that he is someone Millicent can trust? Why or why not?

◆ Drawing Conclusions About Serling's Work

One critic has said that Rod Serling's main themes were "isolation, bigotry, and the double-edge of our choices," and pointed out that Serling's writing was popular and serious at the same time. It "entertained and often startled, but also made viewers think."

Apply these ideas to "Requiem for a Heavyweight" and "The Mirror Image" by filling out the following chart:

	REQUIEM FOR A HEAVYWEIGHT	THE MIRROR IMAGE
How and why main character feels isolated		
How main character reaches out		
How story conflict resolves		

After you fill out your chart, use the information in it to write a short essay in which you compare and contrast the main characters and their dilemmas. In what ways are they similar and different?

◆ Idea Bank

Writing

1. **Glossary** In "Requiem for a Heavyweight," McClintock and Army use boxing terms such as *ringside, heavyweight,* and *punchy.* Make a glossary defining these terms, as well as other boxing terms such as *knockout, down for the count, main event, one-two punch, on the ropes, saved by the bell, pull one's punches,* and *in one's corner.* Explain any terms that now have meanings outside the boxing ring.
2. **Television Script** Rewrite a scene from "The Mirror Image" as a television script, using the same format used in "Requiem for a Heavyweight." For dialogue, write the character's name in capital letters, followed by a colon and then his or her words. Delete the narration, or adapt it as stage directions.
3. **New Ending** What might have happened if Millicent had boarded the

bus or if Paul hadn't called the police? Write a new ending for "The Mirror Image." Your ending can be spooky, humorous, or down-to-earth, but it should follow logically from the characters and situation that Serling has established.

Speaking and Listening

4. Performance With partners, perform a scene from "The Mirror Image" or "Requiem for a Heavyweight." Before your performance, assign roles and discuss how each character in the scene should speak and behave. Practice your scene, and then perform it for the class. **[Performing Arts Link]**

Researching and Representing

5. Multimedia Report Early in Serling's career, original television comedies and dramas were performed and broadcast live. Research other important writers, performers, and shows from television's Golden Age. Then prepare an oral report on this period, using audio and video clips to make the period come alive for your classmates. You may wish to focus on a single show or performer, or on a particular aspect of 1950's

broadcasting, such as the role of advertising. **[Media Link]**

◆ Further Reading, Listening, and Viewing

- Serling, Rod. *Patterns: Four Television Plays with the Author's Personal Commentaries* (1957). This volume includes Serling's scripts for "Requiem for a Heavyweight" and "Patterns," along with his commentary on each play.

- *Twilight Zone 5: The Monsters Are Due on Maple Street* (1993). (Audiocassette). An audio performance of one of the most famous *Twilight Zone* episodes.

- *The Twilight Zone* (1999). (Videocassettes). Memorable episodes of this classic series are now available on video, with three episodes per tape.

- *Rod Serling: Submitted for Your Approval* (1995). (Videocassette). This tribute to the "dazzling visionary" Rod Serling was produced for the PBS series *American Masters.*

On the Web:

http://www.phschool.com/atschool/literature
Go to the student edition *Bronze*. Proceed to Unit 8. Then click Hot Links to find Web sites featuring Rod Serling.

$\mathcal{P}$at Mora In Depth

> "I am interested in how we save languages and traditions. What we have inside of our homes and our families is a treasure chest that we don't pay attention to."
>
> — *Pat Mora*

PAT MORA has written many award-winning essays and poems about her experiences as a Mexican American. She uses rich sensory language to share her observations and communicate her unique perspective. "I take pride in being a Hispanic writer," she says. By sharing her heritage, Mora voices the feelings, experiences, and dreams not only of Mexican Americans, but of all people who grew up on the border of two worlds.

A Childhood in Two Cultures Mora was born in El Paso, Texas, a city located on the border between Mexico and the United States. In the early 1900's, her grandparents migrated to El Paso to escape the revolution in Mexico. As she grew up, Mora and her family frequently visited the Mexican city of Juarez, just across the border from El Paso. As a child, the two cities blurred in her mind to become one large, diverse home.

Mora was raised in a bilingual home—she and her family spoke both Spanish and English. Her parents opened their home to members of their extended family, including Mora's grandmother and her beloved aunt, nicknamed *Lobo,* or wolf. Family stories and customs enriched Mora's life, contributing to her sense of belonging to two worlds: the United States and Mexico.

Trying to Fit In Growing up in two worlds was sometimes difficult for Mora. As she became older, she learned that some people treated Mexicans with little respect. At school, she often hid her ability to speak Spanish to prevent others

from treating her with scorn. Later, she recognized the sadness of this decision, and realized that hiding her Spanish heritage was hiding an important part of herself. She now takes great pride in her dual perspective. "I make it a point to stress my heritage and the fact that I'm bilingual," she says.

Life After High School After attending university in Texas, Mora dedicated herself to helping others learn. She taught middle school, high school, and college students in El Paso.

She also married and raised three children, William, Elizabeth, and Cecilia. After a divorce in 1981, Mora began seriously to consider her life as a writer. She wrote her first two collections of poetry to celebrate her Southwestern heritage, the strong women in her life, and her connections to nature. Her first collection, *Chants,* was published in 1984.

Uncharted Territory Mora believes that one reason she did not start writing sooner was that she had few models to follow. "I'd never seen a writer who was like me, bilingual, Mexican American." She hopes that her writing will inspire others to write, thereby increasing the amount of Mexican American literature that is published. "Anthologized American literature does not reflect the ethnic diversity of the United States," she says. "I write, in part, because Hispanic perspectives need to be part of our literary heritage."

Sources of Inspiration Books were always a fundamental part of Mora's life. She says, "I am a writer because I was always a reader. I love words and their power to move us, to entertain us, to make us laugh, to comfort us."

Mora's family experiences, such as the time her Aunt Lobo danced on her ninetieth birthday, have inspired many of her poems and essays. The powerful desert landscape has also energized her creativity. "Many of my book ideas come from the desert where I grew up," she notes. "The open spaces, wide sky, all that sun and all those animals that scurry across the hot sand or fly high over the mountains."

Beyond the Desert Traveling beyond the Southwest expanded Mora's range of experiences. In her third collection of poetry, *Communion,* she described places as distant as Cuba, New York, and India.

In 1989, Mora moved from El Paso to Cincinnati, Ohio, and the transition was both difficult and enriching. Mora missed the desert landscapes of her youth, but gained deep insights into the United States interior. Today, Mora divides her time between Cincinnati, where she is a professor at the University of Cincinnati, and Santa Fe, New Mexico.

The Writer's Life Mora is a disciplined writer who maintains a regular writing schedule. She works hard to overcome the problems faced by all freelance writers, such as gaining financial security, but she feels that her greatest challenge comes from within. "Personally, the hardest thing about being a writer is facing the gap between what I hope to write and what I write. I'm not talking about quantity because I'm very disciplined, but about how a piece of writing is seldom as effective as we want. We want those words to fly right off the page into the reader's heart."

◆ Bilingualism

Like many Americans, Pat Mora is bilingual; in other words, she is capable of speaking in two languages. Mora says she is "English dominant," meaning that she feels more confident expressing herself in English than in Spanish. She loves the Spanish language, though, and she cherishes her ability to view the world from two language perspectives.

Theories on bilingualism differ, but most experts agree that people who speak more than one language can think in each one. They do not need to "translate" from one language into the other.

One intriguing aspect of speaking multiple languages is the idea that language can shape our thoughts. Many bilingual people feel that they form different ideas or impressions depending on the language in which they are thinking. Some authors say they form ideas in one language and then write about them in another.

Sharing the experience of being bilingual with readers can be difficult. Mora writes almost exclusively in English, though she did write a Spanish ballad in memory of her father. She includes many Spanish terms in order to evoke the specific sounds and phrases of her Mexican heritage, and she takes care to provide translations for readers who do not speak Spanish.

◆ Literary Works

Poetry Collections

- *Chants* (1984, second edition 1994)
- *Borders* (1986, second edition 1993)
- *Communion* (1991)
- *Agua Santa/Holy Water* (1995)
- *Aunt Carmen's Book of Practical Saints* (1999)
- *My Own True Name: New and Selected Poems For Young Adults, 1984–1999* (2000)

Nonfiction

- *Nepantla: Essays from the Land in the Middle* (1993)
- *House of Houses* (1997)

The Border: A Glare of Truth

I moved away for the first time from the U.S.-Mexican border in the fall of 1989. Friends were sure I'd miss the visible evidence of Mexico's proximity[1] found in cities such as my native El Paso. Friends smiled that I'd soon be back for *good* Mexican food, for the delicate taste and smell of *cilantro*, for soft tortillas freshly made. There were jokes about care packages flying to the Midwest.

Although most of my adult home and work life had been spent speaking English, I was prepared to miss the sound of Spanish weaving in and out of my days like the warm aroma from a familiar bakery. I knew I'd miss the pleasure of moving back and forth between two languages—a pleasure that can deepen human understanding and increase our versatility conceptually[2] as well as linguistically.[3]

And indeed, when I hear a phrase in Spanish in a Cincinnati restaurant, my head turns quickly. I listen, silently wishing to be part of that other conversation, if only for a few moments, to feel Spanish in my mouth. I'm reading more poetry in Spanish, sometimes reading the lines aloud to myself, enjoying sounds I don't otherwise hear. Recently I heard a voice on National Public Radio say that learning another language is renaming the world. What an interesting perception. Because language shapes as well as reflects our reality, exploring it allows us to see and to explore our world anew, much as experiencing the world with a young child causes us to pause, savor.

I smile when my children, who were too busy when they were younger, now inform me that when they visit they hope we'll be speaking Spanish. They have discovered as I did that languages are channels, sometimes to other people, sometimes to other views of the world, sometimes to other aspects of ourselves. So we struggle with irregular verbs, laughing together.

Is it my family—children, parents, siblings, niece, nephews— that I miss in this land of leaves so unlike my bare desert? Of course, but my family, although miles away, is with me daily. The huge telephone bills and the steady stream of letters and cards are a long-distance version of the web of caring we once created around kitchen tables. Our family web just happens to stretch across these United States, a sturdy, elastic web steadily maintained by each in his or her own way.

Oh, I miss the meals seasoned with that family phrase, "Remember the time when . . . ?" But I've learned through the

1. **proximity:** Nearness.
2. **conceptually:** Theoretically; related to ideas.
3. **linguistically:** Related to words.

years to cherish our gatherings when I'm in the thick of them, to sink into the faces and voices, to store the memories and stories like the industrious Ohio squirrel outside my window stores her treasures.

I've enjoyed this furry, scurrying companion as I've enjoyed the silence of bare tree limbs against an evening sky, updrafts of snow outside our third-floor window, the ivory light of cherry blossoms. I feel fortunate to be experiencing the geographical center of this country, which astutely[4] calls itself the Heartland. If I'm hearing the "heart," its steady, predictable rhythms, what as I missing from this country's southern border, its margin?

Is it other rhythms? I remember my mixed feelings as a young girl whenever my father selected a Mexican station on the radio, feelings my children now experience about me. I wanted so to *be an American*, which in my mind, and perhaps in the minds of many on the border, meant (and means) shunning anything from Mexico.

But as I grew I learned to like dancing to those rhythms. I learned to value not only the rhythms but all that they symbolized. As an adult, such music became associated with celebrations and friends, with warmth and the sharing of emotions. I revel in a certain Mexican passion not for life or about life, but *in* life—a certain intensity in the daily living of it, a certain abandon in such music, in the hugs, sometimes in the anger. I miss the *chispas*, "sparks," that spring from the willingness, the habit, of allowing the inner self to burst through polite restraints. Sparks can be dangerous but, like risks, are necessary.

I brought cassettes of Mexican and Latin American music with us when we drove to Ohio. I'd roll the car window down and turn the volume up, taking a certain delight in sending such sounds like mischievous imps across fields and into trees. Broadcasting my culture, if you will.

Foreign Spooks

Released full blast into the autumn air
from trumpets, drums, flutes,
the sounds burst from my car like confetti
riding the first strong current.
The invisible imps from Peru, Spain,
Mexico grin as they spring from guitars,
harps, hand claps, and violins,
they stream across the flat fields of Ohio,
hide in the drafts of abandoned gray barns,
and the shutters of stern, white houses,
burrow into cold cow's ears and the crackle

---

4. **astutely:** Smartly.

of dry corn, in squirrel fur, pond ripple, tree gnarl,
owl hollow, until the wind sighs

and they open their wide, impudent
mouths, and together *con gusto*[5]
startle sleeping farm wives,
sashaying raccoons, and even
the old harvest moon.

On my first return visit to Texas, I stopped to hear a group of
mariachis[6] playing their instruments with proud gusto. I was surprised and probably embarrassed when my eyes filled with tears
not only at the music, but at the sight of wonderful Mexican
faces. The musicians were playing from some senior citizens. The
sight of brown, knowing eyes that quickly accepted me with a
smile, the stories in those eyes and in the wrinkled faces were
more delicious than any *fajitas* or *flan*.

When I lived on the border, I had the privilege accorded to a
small percentage of our citizens: I daily saw the native land of my
grandparents. I grew up in the Chihuahua desert, as did they,
only we grew up on different sides of the Rio Grande. That
desert—its firmness, resilience,[7] and fierceness, its whispered
chants and tempestuous[8] dance, its wisdom and majesty—
shaped us as geography always shapes its inhabitants. The
desert persists in me, both inspiring and compelling me to sing
about her and her people, their roots and blooms and thorns.

The desert is harsh, hard as life, no carpet of leaves cushions
a walk, no forest conceals the shacks on the other side of the sad
river. Although a Midwest winter is hard, it ends, melts into rich
soil yielding the yellow trumpeting of daffodils. But the desert in
any season can be relentless as poverty and hunger, realities
prevalent as scorpions in that stark terrain. Anthropologist
Renato Rosaldo, in his provocative challenge to his colleagues,
Culture and Truth, states that we live in a world "saturated with
inequality, power, and domination."

The culture of the border illustrates this truth daily, glaringly.
Children go to sleep hungry and stare at stores filled with toys
they'll never touch, with books they'll never read. Oddly, I miss
that clear view of the difference between my comfortable life and
the lives of so many who also speak Spanish, value family,
music, celebration. In a broader sense, I miss the visible
reminder of the difference between my insulated, economically
privileged life and the life of most of my fellow humans. What I

5. *con gusto* (kōn gōōs´ tō): With pleasure.
6. *mariachis* (mä rē ä´ chēs): Mexican musicians.
7. **resilience:** Flexibility; ability to spring back into shape.
8. **tempestuous:** Stormy.

miss about the sights and sounds of the border is, I've finally concluded, its stern honesty. The fierce light of that grand, wide Southwest sky not only filled me with energy, it revealed the glare of truth.

☑ **Check Your Comprehension**

1. List four things that Mora misses when she moves from El Paso to Ohio.
2. Name two ways in which Mora maintains contact with her El Paso heritage.
3. (a) Describe how Mora feels about the desert. (b) According to Mora, how is the desert like and unlike a Midwest winter?

◆ **Critical Thinking**

INTERPRET

1. Mora explains that her feelings about listening to Mexican music have changed since she was a young girl. What was her original view, and why did it change? **[Analyze Cause and Effect]**
2. How does the poem "Foreign Spooks" express Mora's adult view of Mexican music? **[Interpret]**

EVALUATE

3. Mora says she smiles when her children tell her they want to speak Spanish. Why do you think this makes her happy? **[Infer]**
4. What do you think Mora means when she says that the desert landscape can reveal "the glare of truth"? **[Hypothesize]**

Remembering Lobo

We called her *Lobo*. The word means "wolf" in Spanish, an odd name for a generous and loving aunt. Like all names it became synonymous with her, and to this day returns me to my childself. Although the name seemed perfectly natural to us and to our friends, it did cause frowns from strangers throughout the years. I particularly remember one hot afternoon when on a crowded streetcar between the border cities of El Paso and Juárez, I momentarily lost sight of her. "Lobo! Lobo!" I cried in panic. Annoyed faces peered at me, disappointed at such disrespect to a white-haired woman.

Actually the fault was hers. She lived with us for years, and when she arrived home from work in the evening, she'd knock on our front door and ask, *"¿Dónde estan mis lobitos?"* "Where are my little wolves?"

Gradually she became our lobo, a spinster aunt who gathered the four of us around her, tying us to her for life by giving us all she had. Sometimes to tease her we would call her by her real name. *"¿Dónde esta Ignacia?"*[1] we would ask. Lobo would laugh and say, "She is a ghost."

To all of us in nuclear families[2] today, the notion of an extended family under one roof seems archaic,[3] complicated. We treasure our private space. I will always marvel at the generosity of my parents, who opened their door to both my grandmother and Lobo. No doubt I am drawn to the elderly because I grew up with two entirely different white-haired women who worried about me, tucked me in at night, made me tomato soup or hot *hierbabuena* (mint tea) when I was ill.

Lobo grew up in Mexico, the daughter of a circuit judge, my grandfather. She was a wonderful storyteller and over and over told us about the night her father, a widower, brought his grown daughters on a flatbed truck across the Rio Grande at the time of the Mexican Revolution. All their possessions were left in Mexico. Lobo had not been wealthy, but she had probably never expected to have to find a job and learn English.

When she lived with us, she worked in the linens section of a local department store. Her area was called "piece goods and bedding." Lobo never sewed, but she would talk about materials she sold, using words I never completely understood, such as *pique* and

---

1. *¿Dónde esta Ignacia?* (dōn´ dā es tä´ ēg nä´ sē ä): Where is Ignacia?
2. **nuclear families:** Families that include only parents and their children.
3. **archaic** (är kā´ ik): Old-fashioned; out-of-date.

broadcloth. Sometimes I still whisper such words just to remind myself of her. I'll always savor the way she would order "sweet milk" at restaurants. The precision of a speaker new to the language.

Lobo saved her money to take us out to dinner and a movie, to take us to Los Angeles in the summer, to buy us shiny black shoes for Christmas. Though she never married and never bore children, Lobo taught me much about one of our greatest challenges as human beings: loving well. I don't think she ever discussed the subject with me, but through the years she lived her love, and I was privileged to watch.

She died at ninety-four. She was no sweet, docile Mexican woman dying with perfect resignation. Some of her last words before drifting into semiconsciousness were loud words of annoyance at the incompetence[4] of nurses and doctors.

"No sirven." "They're worthless," she'd say to me in Spanish. "They don't know what they're doing. My throat is hurting and they're taking X-rays. Tell them to take care of my throat first."

I was busy striving for my cherished middle-class politeness. "Shh, shh," I'd say. "They're doing the best they can."

"Well, it's not good enough," she'd say, sitting up in anger.

Lobo was a woman of fierce feelings, of strong opinions. She was a woman who literally whistled while she worked. The best way to cheer her when she'd visit my young children was to ask for her help. Ask her to make a bed, fold laundry, set the table or dry dishes, and the whistling would begin as she moved about her task. Like all of us, she loved being needed. Understandable, then, that she muttered in annoyance when her body began to fail her. She was a woman who found self-definition and joy in visibly showing her family her love for us by bringing us hot *té de canela* (cinnamon tea) in the middle of the night to ease a cough, by bringing us comics and candy whenever she returned home. A life of giving.

One of my last memories of her is a visit I made to her on November 2, *El Día de los Muertos,* or All Souls' Day. She was sitting in her rocking chair, smiling wistfully. The source of the smile may seem a bit bizarre to a U.S. audience. She was fondly remembering past visits to the local cemetery on this religious feast day.

"What a silly old woman I have become," she said. "Here I sit in my rocking chair all day on All Souls' Day, sitting when I should be out there. At the cemetery. Taking good care of *mis muertos,* my dead ones.

"What a time I used to have. I'd wake while it was still dark outside. I'd hear the first morning birds, and my fingers would almost itch to begin. By six I'd be having a hot bath, dressing carefully in black, wanting *mis muertos* to be proud of me, proud to have me looking respectable and proud to have their graves taken care of. I'd

---

4. incompetence: Inadequacy; lack of ability.

have my black coffee and plenty of toast. You know the way I like it. Well browned and well buttered. I wanted to be ready to work hard.

"The bus ride to the other side of town was a long one, but I'd say a rosary[5] and plan my day. I'd hope that my perfume wasn't too strong and yet would remind others that I was a lady.

"The air at the cemetery gates was full of chrysanthemums: that strong, sharp, fall smell. I'd buy tin cans full of the gold and wine flowers. How I like seeing aunts and uncles who were also there to care for the graves of their loved ones. We'd hug. Happy together.

"Then it was time to begin. The smell of chrysanthemums was like a whiff of pure energy. I'd pull the heavy hose and wash the grave-stones over and over, listening to the water pelting away the desert sand. I always brought newspaper. I'd kneel on the few patches of grass, and I'd scrub and scrub, shining the gray stones, leaning back on my knees to rest for a bit and then scrubbing again. Finally a relative from nearby would say, 'Ya, ya, Nacha,' and laugh. Enough. I'd stop, blink my eyes to return from my trance. Slightly dazed, I'd stand slowly, place a can of chrysanthemums before each grave.

"Sometimes I would just stand there in the desert sun and listen. I'd hear the quiet crying of people visiting new graves; I'd hear families exchanging gossip while they worked.

"One time I heard my aunt scolding her dead husband. She'd sweep his gravestone and say, '¿Porqué?[6] Why did you do this, you thoughtless man? Why did you go and leave me like this? You know I don't like to be alone. Why did you stop living?' Such a sight to see my aunt with her proper black hat and her fine dress and her carefully polished shoes muttering away for all to hear.

"To stifle my laughter, I had to cover my mouth with my hands."

I see Lobo in that afternoon sun, and I wonder if the sharp smell of chrysanthemums on her fingertips startled her. Surely she wanted to save it, to save the day, to horde the pleasure of using the love trapped inside all year long. I imagine how she must have enjoyed the feeling of strength in her arms as she scrubbed those graves, loving the notion that her relatives' markers would be the cleanest in the cemetery. They would sparkle.

Bizarre? Bizarre to find happiness in a cemetery? Perhaps, but understanding that attitude toward death—and love—is a key to understanding the growing U.S. Latino population. Family ties are so strong that not even death can sever them. Although Emily Dickinson writes of "sweeping up the Heart / and putting love away / We shall not want to use again / Until Eternity," Mexicans don't always do this. Such tidiness eludes us.

Explanations for such attitudes abound: Indian beliefs of life and death as a continuum, the strong influence of the Catholic

---

5. **rosary:** A group of prayers said with a string of beads.
6. **¿Porqué?** (pôr kā´): Why?

Church with its tenets[7] about the soul and afterlife. Somehow we continue to want to openly demonstrate our love. Lobo's annual cemetery excursions were, yes, a testimony to family pride, but also a testimony to her enduring love for family members.

I wonder if, as she sat before me that last November 2, her arms ached as love pushed against the inside of her skin, trying to find a way out. Her emotional pain at her trapped love, at no longer being able to use her body to help her loved ones—living and dead—was probably as distressing as the physical pain of arthritis. Such capacity for love is as startling as the scent of chrysanthemums.

I have no desire to put my love for Lobo away. Quite the contrary, I don't want to forget: I want to remember. My tribute to her won't be in annual pilgrimages to a cemetery. I was born in these United States and am very much influenced by this culture. But I do want to polish, polish my writing tools to preserve images of women like Lobo, unsung women whose fierce family love deserves our respect. Lobo has been dead almost ten years now. I will always miss her physical presence in my life, her laughter. She's not one to stay out of my life, though. She manages to slip into every book of poetry I write. Her poem for poetry book four is already written, and my first children's book is about her ninetieth birthday party. She danced.

> *Bailando*
>
> I will remember you dancing,
> spinning round and round
> a young girl in Mexico,
> your long, black hair free in the wind,
> spinning round and round
> a young woman at village dances
> your long, blue dress swaying
> to the beat of *La Varsoviana*
> smiling into the eyes of your parents,
> years later smiling into my eyes
> when I'd reach up to dance with you
> my dear aunt, who years later
> danced with my children,
> you, white-haired but still young
> waltzing on your ninetieth birthday,
> more beautiful than the orchid
> pinned on your shoulder,
> tottering now when you walk
> but saying to me, *"Estoy bailando,"*[8]
> and laughing.

---

7. **tenets** (ten´ its): Beliefs.
8. ***Estoy bailando*** (es toi´ bī län´ dō): I am dancing.

Pat Mora

To Gabriela, a Young Writer

The enthusiasm and curiosity of young writers is source of energy. In one sense, we are all fledgling[1] writers. With each new piece, we embark on the mysterious process again, unsure if we can describe or evoke what is in our minds and hearts. Sometimes it is difficult to convince those under thirty that the struggle never ends, that art is not about formulas. Maybe that continuing risk lures us. Luckily, octogenarians[2] such as movie director Akira Kurosawa or Mexican painter Rufino Tamayo show us that we need never retire, and that what we have to share near the end of our lives may be far more lyrical than our early efforts in any art form. A sad truth about art is that it is unlinked to virtue. Wretches can write well while saints produce pedestrian[3] passages.

I like to share what little I know, to encourage beginning writers. When a friend asked if I'd give her thirteen-year-old daughter some advice, I wrote her.

Dear Gabriela,

Your mother tells me that you have begun writing poems and that you wonder exactly how I do it. Do you perhaps wonder why I do it? Why would anyone sit alone and write when she could be talking to friends on the telephone, eating mint chocolate chip ice cream in front of the TV, or buying a new red sweater at the mall?

And, as you know, I like people. I like long, slow lunches with my friends. I like to dance. I'm no hermit, and I'm not shy. So why do I sit with my tablet and pen and mutter to myself?

There are many answers. I write because I'm a reader. I want to give to others what writers have given me, a chance to hear the voices of people I will never meet. Alone, in private. And even if I meet these authors, I wouldn't hear what I hear alone with the page, words carefully chosen, woven into a piece unlike any other, enjoyed by me in a way no other person will, in quite the same way, enjoy them. I suppose I'm saying that I love the privateness of writing and reading. It's delicious to curl into a book.

I write because I'm curious. I'm curious about me. Writing is a way of finding out how I feel about anything and everything. Now that I've left the desert where I grew up, for example, I'm discov-

---

1. **fledgling:** One who is just starting or inexperienced.
2. **octogenarians:** People in their eighties.
3. **pedestrian:** Common, unimaginative.

ering how it feels to walk on spongy fall leaves and to watch snow drifting *up* on a strong wind. I notice what's around me in a special way because I'm a writer, and then I talk to myself about it on paper. Writing is my way of saving my feelings.

I write because I believe that Mexican Americans need to take their rightful place in U.S. literature. We need to be published and to be studied in schools and colleges so that the stories and ideas of our people won't quietly disappear. Although I'm happy when I finish the draft of a poem or story, deep inside I always wish I wrote better, that I could bring more honor and attention to those like the *abuelitas*, grandmothers, I write about. That mix of sadness and pleasure occurs in life, doesn't it?

Although we don't discuss it often because it's depressing, our people have been and sometimes still are viewed as inferior. Maybe you have already felt hurt when someone by a remark or odd look said to you: You're not like us, you're not one of us, speaking Spanish is odd, your family looks funny.

Some of us decide we don't want to be different. We don't want to be part of a group that is often described as poor and uneducated. I remember feeling that way at your age. I spoke Spanish at home to my grandmother and aunt, but I didn't always want my friends at school to know that I spoke Spanish. I didn't like myself for feeling that way. I sensed it was wrong, but I didn't know why. Now, I know.

I know that the society we live in and that the movies, television programs, and commercials we see all affect us. It's not easy to learn to judge others fairly, not because of the car they drive, the house they live in, the church they attend, the color of their skin, the language they speak at home. It takes courage to face the fact that we all have ten toes, get sleepy at night, get scared in the dark. Some families, some cities, some states, and even some countries foolishly convince themselves that they are better than others. And then they teach their children this ugly lie. It's like a weed with burrs and stickers that pricks people.

How are young women who are African American, Asian American, American Indian, Latinas, or members of all the other ethnic groups supposed to feel about themselves? Some are proud of their cultural roots. But commercials are also busy trying to convince us that our car, clothes, and maybe even our family are not good enough. It's so hard today to be your self, your many interesting selves, because billboards and magazines tell you that beautiful is being thin, maybe blonde, and rich, rich, rich. No wonder we don't always like ourselves when we look in the mirror.

There are no secrets to good writing. Read. Listen, Write. Read. Listen. Write. You learn to write well by reading wonderful writing and by letting those words and ideas become part of your blood and bones. But life is not all books. You become a better writer by listening—to your self and to all the colors, shapes, and sounds around you. Listen with all of your senses. Listen to wrinkles on your *tia's*, your aunt's, face.

Writers write. They don't just talk about writing just as dancers don't just talk about dancing. They do it because they love it and because they want to get better and better. They practice and practice to loosen up just as you practiced and practiced when you were learning to talk. And because you practiced, you don't talk the way you did when you were three.

Do you know the quotation that says that learning to write is like learning to ice-skate? You must be willing to make a fool of yourself. Writers are willing to try what they can't do well so that one day they can write a strong poem or novel or children's book.

After a writer gains some confidence, she begins to spend more and more time revising, just as professional ice-skaters create and practice certain routines until they have developed their own, unique style. You probably don't like rewriting now. I didn't either until a few years ago.

How or why a book or poem starts varies. Sometimes I hear a story I want to save, sometimes it's a line, or an idea. It would be as if you saw someone dance and you noticed a step or some special moves and for a few days you didn't actually try the steps, but off and on you thought about them. Maybe you even feel the moves inside you. And then one day you just can't stand it anymore and you turn on the music and begin to experiment. You don't succeed right away, but you're having fun even while you're working to get the rhythm right. And slowly you loosen up, and pretty soon you forget about your feet and arms, and you and the music are just moving together. Then the next day you try it again, and maybe alter it slightly.

My pen is like that music. Usually I like to start in a sunny spot with a yellow, lined tablet and a pen. I have a number of false starts like you did dancing. I'm working but having fun. Alone. The first line of a poem is sometimes a hard one because I want it to be an interesting line. It may be the only line a reader will glance at to decide whether to read the whole piece. I'm searching for the right beginning. I play a little game with myself. (This game works with any kind of writing.) I tell myself to write any line no matter how bad or dull, because I can later throw it away. If I sit waiting for the perfect line, I might never write the poem. I'm willing to make a fool of myself. So I start, usually slowly. I write a few lines, read them aloud, and often start again. I keep sections I like and discard the uninteresting parts. The next day I read my work and try to improve it. I'm trying to pull out of myself the poem or story that's deep inside. It's important not to fall in love with the words you write. Pick your words or phrases, and then stand back and look at your work. Read it out loud.

You and I are lucky to be writers. So many women in history and even today who could be much better writers than I am have not had that private pleasure of creating with words. Maybe their families think writing is a waste of time, maybe they don't believe in themselves, maybe they have to work hard all day and then have to cook and clean and take care of their children at night, maybe they've never been taught to read and write.

I hope that you develop pride in being Mexican American and that you discover what you have to say that no one else can say. I hope that you continue writing, Gabriela.

☑ Check Your Comprehension

1. What is an extended family?
2. How does Lobo take care of her relatives on All Souls' Day?
3. Why does Mora write to Gabriela?
4. What advice does Mora give about rewriting?

◆ Critical Thinking

INTERPRET
1. In what ways does Lobo live up to the meaning of her nickname? **[Analyze]**
2. How does Mora feel about her aunt's dancing at her ninetieth birthday party?

Choose a line from "Bailando" to support your answer. **[Infer]**
3. In "To Gabriela, a Young Writer," Mora compares writing and dancing. How does she believe these activities are similar? **[Compare and Contrast]**
4. Why does Mora encourage Gabriela to be proud of her Mexican American heritage? **[Draw Conclusions]**

COMPARE LITERARY WORKS
5. Choose one piece of advice about writing from "To Gabriela, a Young Writer." Explain how Mora follows this advice in "Remembering Lobo." **[Connect]**

Pat Mora

Same Song

While my sixteen-year-old son sleeps,
my twelve-year-old daughter
stumbles into the bathroom at six a.m.
plugs in the curling iron
5   squeezes into faded jeans
curls her hair carefully
strokes Aztec Blue shadow on her eyelids
smooths Frosted Mauve blusher on her cheeks
outlines her mouth in Neon Pink
10   peers into the mirror, mirror on the wall
frowns at her face, her eyes, her skin,
not fair.

At night this daughter
stumbles off to bed at nine
15   eyes half-shut while my son
jogs a mile in the cold dark
then lifts weights in the garage
curls and bench presses
expanding biceps, triceps, pectorals,
20   one-handed push-ups, one hundred sit-ups
peers into that mirror, mirror and frowns too.

for Libby

Stubborn Woman

You know her.
She keeps walking.

Even at eighty
when her knees ache
5   and she needs a winter coat in May,
she keeps walking.

Even when her ankles swell,
her bones frail fingernails,
her heart uphill
10   louder than car horns,
she keeps walking.

She buys thick heels, takes slow steps,
her pale eyes still gauging the safe route.
She pushes her grumbling body on.
15   She tells it:
we can browse stores whenever we want.
We can buy Listerine, mints, that new hand
cream that removes wrinkles, cologne
if it's on sale.

Pat Mora

Divisadero Street, San Francisco

I watch a woman play with light,
at ease with the loud
orange of nasturtiums[1] running
unchecked among the prim-
5 rose and the purple bursts of lillies of the Nile
in the cement heart of the city,
at ease with the sprawl of cats
and children wherever she kneels;
a woman who starts trees from seeds,
10 smells memories: the scent
of frilled rose geraniums becomes
the bubble-pop of apple jelly
she once scented with such frills. She sniffs
the pollen-heavy air for last year's bees.
15 *Lost without dirt,* she says,
so she greens this hidden square.

Light, ignored by the four straight backs
of buildings, gathers and shimmers
on the faces of daisies and poppies
20 open to the throat, light   dazzles
until we too shimmer.

Callas[2] offer tall flutes of soothing cream.
I watch the woman, a tender
of possibilities, daily squeeze
25 one more stem into her plot.

---

1. nasturtiums (nə stur´ shəms): Garden plants with shield-shaped leaves and
showy, trumpet-shaped, usually red, yellow, or orange spurred flowers.
2. callas: Tall, deep-throated flowers of the lily family, often white or off-white.

A Voice

Even the lights on the stage unrelenting
as the desert sun couldn't hide the other
students, their eyes also unrelenting,
students who spoke English every night

5   as they ate their meat, potatoes, gravy.
Not you. In your house that smelled like
rose powder, you spoke Spanish formal
as your father, the judge without a courtroom

in the country he floated to in the dark
10   on a flatbed truck. He walked slow
as a hot river down the narrow hall
of your house. You never dared to race past him,

to say, "Please move," in the language
you learned effortlessly, as you learned to run,
15   the language forbidden at home, though your mother
said you learned it to fight with the neighbors.

You liked winning with words. You liked
writing speeches about patriotism and democracy.
You liked all the faces looking at you, all those eyes.
20   "How did I do it?" you ask me now. "How did I do it

when my parents didn't understand?"
The family story says your voice is the voice
of an aunt in Mexico, spunky as a peacock.
Family stories sing of what lives in the blood.

25   You told me only once about the time you went
to the state capitol, your family proud as if
you'd been named governor. But when you looked
around, the only Mexican in the auditorium,

you wanted to hide from those strange faces.
30   Their eyes were pinpricks, and you faked
hoarseness. You, who are never at a loss
for words, felt your breath stick in your throat

like an ice-cube. "I can't," you whispered.
"I can't." Yet you did. Not that day but years later.
35   You taught the four of us to speak up.
This is America, Mom. The undo-able is done

in the next generation. Your breath moves
through the family like the wind
moves through the trees.

☑ Check Your Comprehension

1. What makes both the son and daughter frown in "Same Song"?
2. How does the title character of "Stubborn Woman" move?
3. What does the woman on Divisadero Street create?
4. Whom does the speaker address in "A Voice"?
5. In "A Voice," what happened when the speaker's mother went to the state capitol?

◆ Critical Thinking

INTERPRET

1. In "Same Song," what similarity does the speaker notice between her son and daughter? **[Compare]**

2. What does the list of shopping items at the end of "Stubborn Woman" suggest about the title character's personality? **[Infer]**
3. What does Mora mean when she says that she watches "a woman play with light" on Divisadero Street? **[Interpret]**
4. Reread the final sentence in "A Voice." (a) What two things does Mora compare? (b) In what ways are they similar? **[Interpret]**

COMPARE LITERARY WORKS

5. Each of these poems includes at least one female character. Why do you think Mora is drawn to write about women? **[Speculate]**
6. Explain one way in which the stubborn woman in the poem is similar to Aunt Lobo. **[Connect]**

Comparing and Connecting the Author's Works

◆ Literary Focus: Sensory Language

Sensory language appeals to the senses, that is, to your sense of sight, sound, taste, smell, or touch. Writers of poetry, fiction, and nonfiction use sensory language to bring an image or scene to life.

In both her essays and her poetry, Mora shares her experiences by using vivid sensory language. The chart below contains some examples.

Sight	"...the loud orange of nasturtiums running/unchecked among the primrose and the purple bursts of lilies of the Nile/in the cement heart of the city" "Divisadero Street, San Francisco"
Sound	"The family story says your voice is the voice/of an aunt in Mexico, spunky as a peacock." "A Voice"
Taste	"...I'd soon be back for *good* Mexican food, for the delicate taste and smell of cilantro, for soft tortillas freshly made." "The Border"
Smell	"The smell of chrysanthemums was like a whiff of pure energy." "Remembering Lobo"
Touch	"Our family web just happens to stretch across these United States, a sturdy, elastic web steadily maintained by each in his or her own way." "The Border"

Writers do not always address only one sense at a time. By appealing to several senses, a writer can create a marvelous and memorable image. Pat Mora appeals to many senses when she describes the desert and "its firmness, resilience, and fierceness, its whispered chants and tempestuous dance, its wisdom and majesty."

1. To what senses does Mora appeal when she describes "the sound of Spanish weaving in and out of my days like the warm aroma from a familiar bakery"?
2. Find two examples of sensory language in the poem "Bailando" included in "Remembering Lobo." Organize them in a chart like the one to the left.
3. How does Mora use sensory language to create a vivid portrait in "Stubborn Woman"?
4. Name one sensory image from Mora's work that you find particularly effective. Explain why this image appeals to you.

◆ Drawing Conclusions About Pat Mora's Work

Pat Mora often writes about the importance of preserving one's cultural heritage. The sunburst diagram below identifies some of the cultural ideas Mora keeps alive in "Remembering Lobo."

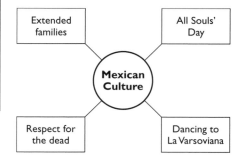

Create a sunburst diagram for "The Border." At the center of the sunburst, write *Mexican Memories*. Review the essay to find details of Mora's life that reflect her Mexican heritage. After completing your diagram, write a paragraph summarizing the cultural memories that Mora wants to keep alive.

◆ Idea Bank

Writing

1. **Letter** Write a letter from Gabriela to Pat Mora, responding to her advice and encouragement. Choose at least two specific lines from Mora's letter, and explain how they affect you.
2. **Memoir** Write a one-page essay about a relative or other person who has been a strong influence on you. Choose two or three specific events that you feel highlight this person's characteristics. Use "Remembering Lobo" as a model.
3. **Poem of Observation** Write a poem that presents your observation of a person you do not know. Use "Stubborn Woman" or "Divisadero Street, San Francisco" as a model. Jot down ideas in a notebook as you observe your subject. Then write your poem, using strong sensory language to bring the person to life.

Speaking, Listening, and Viewing

4. **Music Appreciation** Play a song for your class that reflects something important about your heritage, family, or background. In a group discussion, explain why the song is meaningful to you, and encourage your classmates to share their responses to the music. **[Music Link; Group Activity]**
5. **Illustration** Create an illustration to accompany one of Pat Mora's essays or poems. Make a drawing or painting, or create a collage using photographs from magazines. Display your work, and see whether your classmates can tell which essay or poem the artwork illustrates. **[Art Link]**

Researching and Representing

6. **Visual Report** Growing up on the border between Mexico and the United States had a great influence on Pat Mora and her writing. With a partner, choose two neighboring countries and research the relationship between them. Create a map showing the modern border and a timeline showing important events in the border's history. **[Social Studies Link; Art Link]**
7. **Poll** Conduct a survey to find out which languages are spoken by members of your school or community. Ask also about the languages spoken by each person's parents and grandparents. Create a chart or graph that displays your poll results, and share it with your class. **[Math Link]**

◆ Further Reading, Listening, and Viewing

- *My Own True Name: New and Selected Poems For Young Adults, 1984–1999* (2000). Mora collects poems for young adult readers, hoping that readers will "write their own poems and enjoy the word-play as I do."
- *Nepantla: Essays from the Land in the Middle* (1993). This collection of lectures, speeches, poems, and recollections explores Mora's discovery of herself and the world around her.
- *House of Houses* (1997). This book presents a warm memoir about Mora's extended family.

On the Web:

http://www.phschool.com/atschool/literature
Go to the student edition of *Bronze*. Proceed to Unit 9. Then, click Hot Links to find web sites featuring Pat Mora.

Virginia Hamilton In Depth

"I write books because I love chasing after a good story and seeing fantastic characters rising out of the mist of my imaginings."

—*Virginia Hamilton*

VIRGINIA HAMILTON is a storyteller who composes fascinating tales that often combine historical and fantastical elements. Drawing on her African American heritage, Hamilton writes short stories, novels, and essays that challenge and intrigue young readers. Hamilton says she never starts writing by trying to make a point or accomplish a specific goal. "That's not how you write a book," she explains. "You're not trying to 'accomplish' anything, but tell a good story, and my books are full of good stories."

Growing Up on a Farm Virginia Hamilton was born in Yellow Springs, Ohio, in 1936. She grew up on a farm that was founded by her mother's father, Levi Perry, who escaped from slavery on the Underground Railroad.

Daily life on the farm was difficult, but also joyous. Hamilton remembers childhood as a tremendously happy time, a fact that influenced her decision to write for young readers. "I write for children (and their older allies)," says Hamilton, "because I have such clear memories about being a kid."

A Family of Storytellers Another strong influence on Hamilton's writing career was her family's love of stories. "I grew up within the warmth of loving aunts and uncles, all reluctant farmers but great storytellers," she says. Her grandfather's story about his escape from slavery aroused pride and amazement in young Virginia every time she heard it.

Launching a Writer's Career From an early age, Hamilton knew she wanted to write. After earning full scholarships and studying at Antioch College and Ohio State University, she moved to New York City. There, she continued her study of writing and absorbed the artistic life of the city.

At first, Hamilton and her husband, the poet Arnold Adoff, struggled to make ends meet. In addition to writing, she worked at such varied jobs as cost accountant for an engineering firm, nightclub singer, and museum receptionist. Acceptance as a writer came slowly for her.

Then, in 1967, Hamilton's life changed in several ways. She published her first novel, *Zeely*, to wide acclaim. It was an unusually successful first novel, partly because of its realistic portrayal of African American characters. She also moved with her husband and two children back to Yellow Springs, Ohio.

Heritage and Heroes In her next novel, *The House of Dies Drear* (1968), Hamilton wrote a modern mystery about a house that was once a station on the Underground Railroad.

After that, Hamilton continued to write novels that combine genres and explore elements of African American history. She also began to collect and retell the tales she heard as a child. She selected her favorites and shared them in collections such as *The People Could Fly: American Black Folktales* (1985) and *In the Beginning: Creation Stories From Around the World* (1988).

Recognition and Awards Hamilton has received almost every major award in the field of children's literature, including the Hans Christian Andersen Medal, the Laura Ingalls Wilder Medal, and an

NAACP Image Award. She has received the Coretta Scott King award four times.

In 1974, her novel *M.C. Higgins, the Great* was the first book to win both the Newbery Medal and the National Book Award. This realistic novel tells how the Higgins family home is endangered by a nearby strip-mining company. Poet Nikki Giovanni admired the novel's realistic vision. She wrote, "*M.C. Higgins, the Great* is not an adorable book, not a lived-happily-ever-after kind of story. It is warm, humane and hopeful and does what every book should do—creates characters with whom we can identify and for whom we care."

◆ **Tales From Slavery**

Virginia Hamilton has always been fascinated by the tales told by African Americans during the period of slavery in the United States. These tales include first-hand accounts of slave life, folk tales told among slaves, and tales of escape.

Hamilton believes that accounts of slavery can help readers understand what it felt like to be deprived of freedom and forced to work. For this reason, she believes, it is important to pass on tales from this tragic period of African American history.

The folk tales told by African American slaves are often variations of tales first told in Africa. Many of these tales involve animals, such as rabbits, foxes, bears, wolves, turtles, or snakes. The tales, which feature animals who are given human characteristics, often take place on plantations. A particularly popular animal is the clever rabbit, known as B'rabby, or Brer, Buh, or Bruh Rabbit.

Slaves also told tales about human characters. Despite the harshness of the slaves' lives, these tales are often highly comic. Listeners may have drawn strength and courage from the ability of the stories to find humor in tragedy.

◆ **Literary Works**

Novels
- *Zeely* (1967)
- *The House of Dies Drear* (1968)
- *The Planet of Junior Brown* (1971)
- *M. C. Higgins, the Great* (1974)
- *Arilla Sun Down* (1976)
- *The Justice Trilogy* (1978–1981)
- *Sweet Whispers, Brother Rush* (1982)
- *Willie Bea and the Time the Martians Landed* (1983)
- *The Magical Adventures of Pretty Pearl* (1983)
- *A Little Love* (1984)
- *Junius Over Far* (1985)
- *The Mystery of Drear House: The Conclusion of the Dies Drear Chronicle* (1987)
- *Cousins* (1990)
- *Plain City* (1993)
- *Second Cousins* (1998)
- *Bluish* (1999)

Biography and Nonfiction
- *W.E.B. DuBois* (1972)
- *Paul Robeson* (1974)
- *Anthony Burns: The Defeat and Triumph of a Fugitive Slave* (1988)
- *Many Thousand Gone: African Americans From Slavery to Freedom* (1992)

Story Collections
- *The People Could Fly: American Black Folktales* (1985)
- *In the Beginning: Creation Stories From Around the World* (1988)
- *The Dark Way: Stories From the Spirit World* (1990)
- *The All Jahdu Story Book* (1991)
- *Her Stories: African American Folk Tales, Fairy Tales, and True Tales* (1995)
- *Jaguarundi* (1995)
- *When Birds Could Talk and Bats Could Sing: The Adventures of Bruh Sparrow, Sis Wren, and Their Friends* (1995)
- *A Ring of Tricksters: Animal Tales From America, the West Indes, and Africa* (1997)

Bruh Alligator and Bruh Deer

Long time, nothin here but animal and bird and the Indian. Bruh Alligator and Bruh Deer not any kind of friends atall. Bruh Alligator even plan to kill Bruh Deer when he get the chance. And Bruh Deer very afraid to swim cross the river. Whenever he go down to the river edge for a drink, he cock his head, listenin, and look all around him before he do drink. Just so scared, he, of Bruh Alligator.

By and by comes the *buckras*, the white owners. And then comes the black slaves; and by and by, the *buckras* fetch the hounds. And then the Indian is gone and the *buckras* come to hunt Bruh Deer with they English beagle hounds. They dogs, they beagle hounds, they so swift and they tryin to get so close to Bruh Deer. Only chance Bruh Deer has is to take to the water. But who in the water? Bruh Alligator, who. Nothin matter to Bruh Deer. He have to make for the water when the hounds come too close.

Now the first time the *buckras* run Bruh Deer with the hounds, he didn't know nothin about them. And he just lie down in his bed in the thicket on the edge of the broom-grass field. But here come the hounds, and Bruh Deer so afraid and so, he jump and he run. And he gets away to the river first. Just as he ready to jump off the bluff above the river, he look down and see Bruh Alligator's two big eyes come risin out of the water. Bruh Alligator just waitin for him!

That alligator hungry. Vittles[1] very scarce that time a season. His belly be pinchin him hard, now. But Bruh Deer is fat, and so he is in heavy trouble. The alligator there in front of him. The beagles there behind him. What Bruh Deer done do? He sees the alligator and he hears the beagles.

Bruh Deer make a sudden twist to the side just before the hounds see him. He burn the wind down the riverbank below the bluff, and he cross the water where Bruh Alligator never see him.

Here come the beagles boilin hard for the bluff. They come so fast upon Bruh Deer's track, they never have a chance to stop. Two or three go on over the bluff, and they drop in the water right in front of Bruh Alligator's snout.

Bruh Alligator think to heself, What this here? I never seen such animals before. But it's vittles! Food! And he grabs one, two of the beagles and pulls them under the water. The other hound swum out of there, took he feet in he hands, and ripped on home.

Well, Bruh Deer got away that time. He gone! And when he ready to cross that river again, he look around for Bruh Alligator

---

1. **Vittles:** Food.

first. He find him, too. Bruh Alligator stretched out on a mud-bank in the sunhot. He got a belly full of beagle and he satisfy with heself. He sound asleep. And Bruh Deer sneak close to the river to take a chance on gettin across.

Before Bruh Deer can wet he hoof, Bruh Alligator see him and he slip off the bank to go meet Bruh Deer. How Bruh Deer gone get across go see his family? Before he even thinkin about it, Bruh Alligator start a-talkin.

"Brutha," Bruh Alligator say, "this thing that I ate they call beagle is very good vittles. I love eatin him very much, too. He so easy to catch, and he got no horns to scratch my throat."

"Well, if you love eatin him so and you want to catch him so, will you leave me and my family alone?" Bruh Deer ask him.

Bruh Alligator answer, "I can't catch the beagle less he fall in the river. So let's you, me, make a greement to last as long as this river run."

"What is the greement?" ask Bruh Deer.

"Here tis," says Bruh Alligator. "When you take to the river, I'll take the beagle what chasin you. Me for you, and you for me, and both us for one another."

So Bruh Deer say it all right with him.

And that how it been since the greement made. Whenever hounds run Bruh Deer, Bruh Deer take to the river and Bruh Alligator leave him alone. The hound gone track Deer, and Alligator gone get hound.

But if Bruh Deer ever come to the river without the dogs chasin him, then he have to take he chance.

This tale is translated from the Gullah dialect. In Gullah, the last two paragraphs of the tale above would read: "Dat w'ymekso ebbuh sence de' 'greement mek, w'enebbuh dog run'um, buh deer tek de ribbuh en' buh alligettuh lem'lone, en' w'en de beagle' come 'e ketch'um, but ef buh deer ebbuh come duh ribbuh bidout dog dey att'um, him haffuh tek 'e chance."

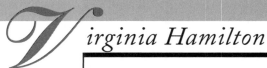

Bruh Lizard and Bruh Rabbit

Don't know some animal tells. Hear um but forget um. Do know about Bruh Lizard and Bruh Rabbit, though. You never hear um tell how Bruh Lizard bested Bruh Rabbit? Well, that lizard was a hard worker. He had a big sword he use to cut his crop. Sword knew how to work by heself and it cut so fine, there was nothin left, once somethin was cut. Bruh Lizard speakin words to the sword and Sword do all the work. That's how it went.

Now, Bruh Rabbit, he is smart. He don't have him a sword like the lizard has, and he wants one. So he hides behind a bush and he watches Sword workin for Bruh Lizard. He wants it very bad, too.

One day Bruh Lizard has to go away. And Bruh Rabbit, he sneak up and he steal Bruh Lizard's sword. Bruh Rabbit laughs to heself because he now got Sword. He think he knows the words that Lizard says to Sword, so he calls out, "Go-ee-tell," like that. And Sword starts in workin, just a-cuttin and a-slashin this way and that and all around.

Pretty soon, old Sword finish up the crop and the rabbit want it to stop. Sword is comin very close to the other crop the rabbit is keepin to live on.

So Bruh Rabbit, he yells out to Sword, "Go-ee-tell. Go-ee-tell!" like that. That just make Sword work that much faster. Sword go on and cut down everythin Rabbit have. It don't leave nothin, not one leaf cabbage.

Now Bruh Lizard, he been hidin behind a bush. He sees the whole thing. He is laughin and laughin to heself at Bruh Rabbit, cause that Rabbit think he so smart when he steal Sword. And now Bruh Rabbit got nothin to eat all winter long.

Bruh Rabbit spies the lizard, and he calls over there, "Lizard, Bruh, stop Sword!"

Bruh Lizard, he call right back, "It my Sword."

Bruh Rabbit, he say then, "That's so. It's your Sword, but please stop it. It ain't got no sense. It cut down everythin I got."

Lizard say, "Sword work faster every time he hear 'Go-ee-tell.'" The lizard laughs again, and he calls out real loud, "Go-ee-pom!" Sword stop.

The lizard grinnin to heself all over the place. Then he slide out there and pick up Sword and take it on home.

Rabbit watch him go.

That's all.

A version of a dialect plantation tale from the Georgia Sea Isles. It is a derivation of the numerous magic-hoe motif tales from Africa and Europe. This is one of the few animal tales in which the cunning Bruh Rabbit doesn't come out the winner.

In another version of the magic-hoe tale, Bruh Rabbit and Bruh Wolf are the contestants. The rabbit's saying "Swish, swish" makes the hoe go faster. When the wolf says "Slow, boy," the hoe slows down.

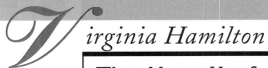

Virginia Hamilton

The Most Useful Slave

Say that John was the most useful slave on the plantation. The slaveowner never havin to worry about his slaves tryin to run away or to startin a bad trouble. He had a way of knowin exactly what was goin on around the plantation. And the way he knew was because of John.

Now John knew how to prophesy for the slaveowner, who was Mas Tom. He could tell you what was gone happen, and he was never wrong once in his predictions. The slaveowner believed John was a fortune-teller with supernatural power. For John knew exactly what the slaveowner wanted done and exactly when he wanted it done, as well.

The truth was that John collected all he needed to know from eavesdroppin, by listenin in on the slaveowner and his wife while they ate their supper.

One day the owner, Tom, was talkin to some other planters, and he found out that they were worried about unrest among the slaves. After listenin awhile, Tom said he never had to worry about anythin because he had a real smart slave who could prophesy.

"There ain't a slave that smart that can foretell," one of the planters said.

"Well, I'll bet you money there is," Tom said.

"You that sure?" the planter asked. And Tom said he was.

"You all put down your money," he told them, "and come over to my house next Sat'dy and you'll see for yourselves."

Well, all the slaveowners put their money down. It came to thousands and thousands of dollars, too. And they all accepted slaveowner Tom's invitation.

Well, the day came. Wasn't a bad day atall. And all the owners came. And they were eager to see this slave that was so smart.

Someone had a place for John to stand. In front of the place one of the planters put a big box. There was something inside it. Nobody knew but the one had put it there what it was.

When everythin seemed to be ready and everybody had gathered around and quieted down, Mas Tom brought John out, blindfolded, and had him stand there.

One of the planters name of Mas Carter said to John, "We're gone see what we see this day, and I got money down on you."

"Well, what for?" blindfolded John says.

"Well, you must know," says the owner Carter. "You the one knows everythin."

Just then, Mas Tom says, "Now, neighbors, Uncle John here will tell us what is hidden in that big box."

Now you know, what was in the big box was a little smaller box so John couldn't hear what was goin on inside.

Well, John stood there for a long, long time, tryin to hear at least some scratchin from the box. But he couldn't. But he worked his hands like he swattin the air and gettin somethin in his head that way. He looked to be tranced some way.

John thought and he thought. The more he had to stand there blindfolded, the more he knew he didn't know what was in the big box. He had no idea atall what was in the little smaller box cause he didn't even know it was there.

It's no use, John thought. Guess what I will is in that box, I'd be wrong. "In the box! In the box!" he said out loud. Didn't know he'd said it. But it caused the planters there to get to murmurin, thinkin somethin was about to happen. He'd said "box" twice, and that made the owner Carter take a listen.

And John was figurin he might as well give it up. He scratched his head and shifted his feet around.

"Well, Mas Tom," he said finally, "this old raccoon, he run a long time, but they caught him at last."

When John said that, his owner, Tom, lifted the box and the smaller box. Lo and behold, a raccoon jumped out to the ground.

"Well, thank you, Uncle John!" says his owner. He couldn't've been happier. See, John was a prophet and Mas Tom was a whole bunch richer.

John doesn't get his freedom in this tale, but he will be valued so long as he can continue as "the prophet." This is the best-known of the "old Marster and John (or Jack)" or "old Marster and the slave" tales, of which there are many.

Old Marster, sometimes called Mas, and John tales are found in the southern United States and among East Africans, and Haitians, Jamaicans, Puerto Ricans, and many other Caribbean peoples. The tales are a cycle narrative (tales told one after the other over a period of time), sometimes accompanied by the banjo. They reveal the slave, John, rather than Bruh Rabbit, as the plantation slaves' trickster hero. John and the owner seem to have an almost friendly relationship.

In some of the other John tales, Old Mas is referred to as Boss, which identifies those tales as taking place after slavery and signals the former slave's uneasy relationship with his former owner.

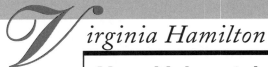

Virginia Hamilton

How Nehemiah Got Free

In slavery time, there was smart slaves and they did most what they wanted to do by usin just their wits. Hangin around the big house, they kept the slaveowners laughin. They had to "bow and scrape" some, but they often was able to draw the least hard tasks.

Nehemiah was a one who believed that if he must be a slave, he'd best be a smart one. No one who callin himself Master of Nehemiah had ever been able to make him work hard for nothin. Nehemiah would always have a funny lie to tell or he made some laughin remark whenever the so-called Master had a question or a scoldin.

Nehemiah was always bein moved from one plantation to another. For as soon as the slaveowner realized Nehemiah was outwittin him, he sold Nehemiah as quick as he could to some other slaveholder.

One day, the man known as the most cruel slaveowner in that part of the state heard about Nehemiah.

"Oh, I bet I can make that slave do what I tell him to," the slaveowner said. And he went to Nehemiah's owner and bargained for him.

Nehemiah's new owner was Mister Warton, and he told Nehemiah, "I've bought you. Now tomorra, you are goin to work for me over there at my plantation, and you are goin to pick four hundred pounds of cotton a day."

"Well, Mas, suh," Nehemiah says, "that's all right, far as it goes. But if I make you laugh, won't you lemme off for tomorra?"

"Well," said Warton, who had never been known to laugh, "if you make me laugh, I won't only let you off for tomorra, but I'll give you your freedom right then and there!"

"Well, I declare, Mas, suh, you sure a good-lookin man," says Nehemiah.

"I'm sorry I can't say the same about you, Nehemiah," answered the slaveowner.

"Oh, yes, Mas, you could," Nehemiah said, laughin. "You could if you told as big a lie as I just did."

Warton threw back his head and laughed. It was a long, loud bellow. He had laughed before he thought. But true is true and facts are facts. And Nehemiah got his freedom.

Folktales about how slaves got their freedom were told in one form or another and are still told in black families all over this country. They are told in the spirit of a Nineteenth of June celebration. That is "Juneteenth," the day on which black people in the South remember Emancipation and give special thanks to freedom from slavery.

Slaves did not learn about Emancipation all at once together. Isolated and scattered all over the South, they heard the extraordinary news at separate times and in different months. But June Nineteenth became the day of freedom for all—Juneteenth. The significance of Juneteenth is very great and gives special meaning to all running-away, enduring-slavery, and end-of-slavery tales.

☑ Check Your Comprehension

1. What agreement do Bruh Alligator and Bruh Deer make?
2. Why can't Bruh Rabbit stop the sword from cutting vegetables?
3. How is John able to convince Mas Tom that he has supernatural abilities?
4. What bargain does Nehemiah make with Mister Warton?

◆ Critical Thinking

INTERPRET

1. In what way is Bruh Alligator's line "Me for you, you for me, and both us for one another" important to "Bruh Alligator and Bruh Deer"? **[Interpret]**
2. The moral of a story is a guide for living that you can apply to your own life. What do you think is the moral of "Bruh Lizard and Bruh Rabbit"? **[Infer]**
3. Explain how John is able to trick Mas Tom and the other owners at the end of "The Most Useful Slave." **[Analyze]**

APPLY

4. Choose one of the tales and explain why you think it was commonly told during the time of slavery. **[Relate]**

Virginia Hamilton
Comparing and Connecting the Author's Works

◆ Literary Focus: Folk Tales

Folk tales, also called **folk literature, folklore,** and **traditional literature,** are stories that communicate the important values or ideas of a culture. Folk tales are composed orally and then passed from person to person by word of mouth. Most folk tales are anonymous: No one knows who first composed them. When modern writers such as Virginia Hamilton retell a folk tale, they try to capture the feeling and spirit of the tale as it has been told for hundreds of years.

In general, the characters in folk tales are simple and have only one major trait, such as honesty, cleverness, or deceitfulness. They are often animals. The characters are usually flat, rather than round. This means that they don't change during the course of the story.

The conflicts in folk tales are often simple and straightforward. For example, in "Bruh Alligator and Bruh Deer," Bruh Deer must figure out a way to prevent Bruh Alligator from attacking him when he drinks from the river. Once the goal is achieved, the story ends quickly. Good usually triumphs over evil.

Folk tales tend to have a lot of repetition. Words, phrases, and events occur more than once, making the key parts easy to remember. In addition, folk tales often contain elements of fantasy or magic.

1. In "Bruh Lizard and Bruh Rabbit," what are the main character traits of the lizard and the rabbit?
2. Are Bruh Lizard and Bruh Rabbit flat or round characters? Use details from the story to support your answers.
3. Name three characteristics of "Bruh Alligator and Bruh Deer" that make it a folk tale.

4. What value do you think "Bruh Alligator and Bruh Deer" teaches readers? What value do you think "Bruh Lizard and Bruh Rabbit teaches readers? Explain your answers.

◆ Drawing Conclusions About Hamilton's Work

Reviewer Ethel Heins said the following about the work of Virginia Hamilton: "Few writers of fiction for young people are as daring, inventive, and challenging to read—or to review—as Virginia Hamilton. Frankly making demands on her readers, she nevertheless expresses herself in a style essentially simple and concise."

Heins's review suggests that Hamilton's style is simple, but her subject matter is challenging and informative. Reread one of her stories with this quote in mind.

After you read, write a paragraph in response to Heins's statement. Give examples of the simplicity of the style, and of the challenging subject matter. Then, explain why you think Hamilton chooses to deal with difficult subject matter in a simple style. Before you write, organize your thoughts in a chart like this one.

Challenging Idea	Simple Way of Expressing It

◆ Idea Bank

Writing

1. **Rewrite in Standard English** Rewrite one of Hamilton's folk tales in standard English. Use standard English spelling and grammar rather than the dialect that Hamilton uses. Then, read your version to a small group and discuss how it affects the story. **[Group Activity]**

2. **Letter to the Author** Write a letter to Virginia Hamilton explaining one thing you learned from reading her work. Describe specific reactions to the stories you have read. Then, share the letter with the class and, if you desire, send it to the author.

3. **Folk Tale** Choose one of the animal characters from Hamilton's tales, and write another folk tale about it. For example, you might write about Bruh Alligator meeting one of the hunter's beagles or Bruh Rabbit getting another chance to steal Bruh Lizard's sword. Use Hamilton's stories as models.

Speaking, Listening, and Viewing

4. **Speech** Imagine that Nehemiah is coming to your school to give a speech about his life. Prepare the speech he would give, including details about how he spent his life after gaining freedom. Then, rehearse the speech and present it to your class.

5. **Reader's Theater** In small groups, adapt "Bruh Alligator and Bruh Deer" or "Bruh Lizard and Bruh Rabbit" so you can present it as Reader's Theatre. Each character should be read by a different actor, and the narration can be read by one or more actor. Rehearse your presentation to become familiar with the dialect and sharpen your characterizations. Then, share your performance with your class. **[Performing Arts Link; Group Activity]**

Researching and Representing

6. **Historical Map** Create a map showing the boundaries between free and slave states before the Civil War. Also, include details about the Underground Railroad on the map and in a paragraph that accompanies it. **[Social Studies Link; Art Link]**

◆ Further Reading, Listening, and Viewing

- *Zeely* (1967). Hamilton's first novel presents an intriguing story about a young girl and her mysterious neighbor.

- *The House of Dies Drear* (1968) and *The Mystery of Drear House: The Conclusion of the Dies Drear Chronicle* (1987). These novels tell about a family that lives in a house that was once a station on the Underground Railroad.

- *In the Beginning: Creation Stories from Around the World* (1988). Twenty-five tales from different cultures explain the origin of the world.

- *Drylongso* (1992). During a dangerous drought, a farm family meets a mysterious boy who knows secrets about finding water.

On the Web:

http://www.phschool.com/atschool/literature
Go to the student edition *Bronze*. Proceed to Unit 10. Then, click Hot Links to find Web sites featuring Virginia Hamilton.

University of Pittsburgh Press
"Pepper Tree" by Gary Soto from *THE ELEMENTS OF SAN JOAQUIN*. Copyright © 1977 Gary Soto.

University Press of New England
"The Gymnast" by Gary Soto from *A SUMMER LIFE*. Copyright © 1990 Gary Soto.

Note: Every effort has been made to locate the copyright owner of material reprinted in this book. Omissions brought to our attention will be corrected in subsequent printings.

Photo Credits

• • • •